WEST INDIES IN YOUR POCKET

WEST INDIES IN YOUR POCKET

A STEP-BY-STEP GUIDE
AND TRAVEL ITINERARY

BY CYNDY & SAM MORREALE

Horizon Books

British Library Cataloguing in Publication Data

Morreale, Cyndy
    West Indies in your pocket: a step-by-step
    guide and travel itinerary — (Pocket travellers)
    1. West Indies — Visitors' guides
    I. Title II. Morreale, Sam III. Series
    917.29'0452

    ISBN 1-85461-030-9

This edition first published in 1989 by Horizon Books Ltd, Harper & Row
House, Estover Road, Plymouth PL6 7PZ, United Kingdom. Tel: Plymouth
(0752) 705251. Telex: 45635. Fax: (0752) 777603.

Typeset by TND Serif, Hadleigh, Ipswich.

Printed in Great Britain by BPCC Wheatons Ltd, Exeter

CONTENTS

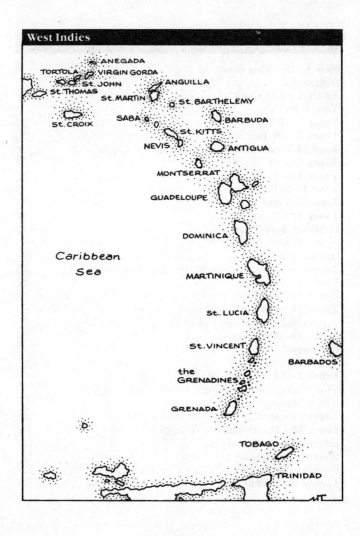

HOW TO USE THIS BOOK

West Indies in Your Pocket is your handy tour guide for the ultimate Caribbean holiday. It's designed for the active traveller rather than the tourist who wants to recline on the same beach for two weeks.

If you yearn to drift beyond the packaged world of big-time tourist resorts, to island-hop among tropical paradises in search of the perfect beach, this book was written with you in mind. Each of its three overlapping travel itineraries shows you the best plan for three weeks of inter-island travel, sightseeing and socialising in a part of the Leeward and Windward Islands. Combine them all and people back home will wonder what ever happened to you.

How to enjoy the West Indies

When we told a friend about the book we were working on, his response was, 'I hated the Caribbean. I'm never going to make that mistake again!' His story was all too typical. His travel agent had booked him into a big resort in the island's most developed tourist area. He worked on his tan for a week and couldn't find anything else to do besides mooch around the resort and go to the disco at night. He had little in common with the resort's other guests. He spent a fortune during his stay—and didn't even have a good time.

The problem had nothing to do with where he went. Lack of variety and change spoiled his holiday. He could have spared himself all that with the help of a more knowledgeable and creative travel agent.

Explaining to our friend that the Caribbean doesn't have to be boring, we realised the need for a book like the one you're holding now.

Variety is the secret of an exciting Caribbean holiday. When one island gets familiar (and they do, some of the more touristy ones by the second day), just hop on a small inter-island passenger plane or mail boat to a completely different place. There's no shortage of possibilities. The West Indies are a kaleidoscope of people, languages, histories and cultures. The array of islands includes tiny independent countries and some of the last remaining European colonies on the face of the earth. Caribbean life is not just a beach. In fact, our favourite little-known island, Saba, has retained its genuine charm partly because it has no beach. Instead, you can wander through a tropical forest, snorkel on colourful reefs that dazzle with thousands of fish, learn to scuba or windsurf, shop in local markets and stay in small guesthouses where you'll meet the people who make the island their home, not just other holidaymakers.

With this book you'll find reggae, rum, crab races, limbo, duty-free shopping, chicken legs (barbecued or curried), 'mountain chicken', roti, tropical rain forests, sailboats and 130-foot yachts, breadfruits and passion fruits, passion, fruits, beach bums, rock stars and the rich, miles of white sand beaches, nude beaches, beach parties, yacht parties, diving and snorkelling, windsurfing, raw conch, walks to breathtaking waterfalls, campsites on remote beaches and mail boats you can ride between islands alongside a goat. Along the way you'll encounter wonderful people as well.

Meeting the locals is vital to full enjoyment of your island vacation. A friendly face far from home can make all the difference, especially in the Caribbean where socialising is more important than sightseeing. That's why we've named many of the wonderful West Indies residents we've come to know during our five years of island-hopping and suggested that you look them up. Given the lazy pace of island life, there's a high probability that they'll still be around when you get there. Tell them Sam and Cyndy sent you.

Island-hopping requires a crash course in saying, 'No problem!' Local people say it a lot, and you should too. In fact, island residents tend to be more relaxed than holiday visitors, so if you expect prompt service and on-time transport you'll encounter frustrations. Though you may rant and rave, islanders will view a rigid schedule as your problem, not theirs. Instead, leave your wristwatch at home and tune in to the easygoing rhythms of life in the tropics. Variety, flexibility and a carefree attitude are the keys to happiness in the Caribbean.

Each section in this guide describes one island. Some are one-day side trips, while others will take several days to explore. For each island you'll find:

1. A **suggested schedule.**
2. Transport information for **getting there** and **getting around.**
3. **Sightseeing highlights** and **activities,** listed in order of our personal preference. (There's no such thing as a 'must-see' attraction in the West Indies, but each one we've included is worth visiting.)
4. **Food** and **accommodation** recommendations.
5. An easy to read **map** of the island.
6. **Helpful hints** and insights to make your visit more enjoyable.

Prices are quoted throughout in sterling approximations with dollars in brackets, assuming £1 = \$1.75, to give you a rough idea of the costs involved. Obviously the exchange rate will vary and guesthouses will put their prices up after publication of this book, so you will need to budget accordingly.

The book presents the islands in the easiest sequence for hopping from one to the next. For the most part you'll be travelling 'down-island', that is, east and south.

When to go

If the winter weather is dreadful you'll be tempted to escape to the tropics in January or February—a reasonable choice if you don't mind spending plenty of money. On the other hand, budget travellers should opt for the summer months. Many people think of the islands as sweltering in summer, but in fact there is very little change in temperature between winter and summer. Tradewinds help keep things cool. Cities can be hotter, but the shores are usually pleasant—and prices are *much* lower.

If you do go when Jack Frost starts nipping at your nose, you'll be just one of the flock heading that way for the winter, by far the heaviest tourist season in the islands. When the 'snow birds' soar in, prices soar as well. Room rates at many hotels double from December 15 to April 15.

Guesthouses, in general, are reasonably priced all year long, but availability varies when the tourist population is heavier. Winter travel can be affordable, but it requires much more advance planning. You'll need to book your accommodation ahead of time to ensure the best value—or plan to pay the difference.

Windjammer Cruises are the same cost year-round, but cruises start filling up around the end of November and stay booked through Easter. Many of the more tourist-oriented islands, such as Antigua and Barbados, get their heavy influx of tourists at the end of November as well.

The West Indies don't really have a 'bad weather' season worth worrying about. Hurricanes are rarely a problem. Modern science gives plenty of warning, and most hurricanes just begin in the islands, travelling to the Gulf of Mexico and Florida before they get fierce. Dominica has been the hardest hit of the islands. Most hurricanes occur in the autumn, though the official season begins on 1 June.

The rainy season is also in the autumn, but even then it doesn't usually rain hard. Residents of islands like Saba who depend on rain to fill their cisterns laugh at the dismayed traveller complaining that his holiday is ruined. 'You call that rain? Why, we didn't even get a ripple in the cistern!' Good heavy rain is a welcome thing in the islands. After skimping on showers for a month, there is a sense of rejoicing when the cistern rises a good six inches.

How much will it cost?

A reasonably frugal couple travelling together can take any of the

island-hopping trips described in this book for about £900 apiece,
or £40 a day ($1,600, or $75 a day), on top of the flight out.
That estimate includes £30 ($50) (double) per night for
guesthouse accommodation, a generous £12 ($20) apiece per day
for food, and an extra £375 ($635) apiece for tours, equipment
hire and incidental expenses. Diehard budget travellers can cut
this 'incidentals' budget considerably by refraining from the
consumption of alcoholic beverages (a sport which, throughout the
Caribbean, is more popular than football).

Transport during your trip will cost upwards from £140 ($250),
depending on the method of travel you choose. For example, if
you follow Itinerary 1, travel from St Croix to St Thomas via
seaplane is £17 ($29); ferries through the Virgins will cost
approximately £10 ($20); it's a £30 ($50) round-trip between
Tortola and Anegada; £25 ($40) one-way from Tortola to St
Martin; £6 ($10) round-trip to Anguilla; £30 ($50) round-trip day
sail to St Barth; and £22 ($40) for the round-trip flight to Saba,
making a grand total of £140 ($250) for inter-island travel. Taxis
and car rentals will add to your transport costs, while discount air
fares may reduce them.

A second possibility: from St Lucia £200 ($350) will cruise you
through the Grenadines on the *Carib Islander,* and a 21-day fare
on Leeward Islands Air Transport (LIAT) airlines will take you
to three more islands and back to St Lucia for just £85 ($149).
Total £285 ($499).

Or: Windjammer offers 7-day cruises at £360 ($625) per person,
including meals and some drinks. You can add the LIAT fare for
£85 ($149) for a grand total of £445 ($774).

Cruising the Grenadines can also be done by mail boat for as
little as £15 ($25) — taking in St Vincent, Bequia, Canouan,
Union Island, Carriacou and Grenada. British West Indies
Airlines (BWIA) allows stopovers on their flights from Barbados
to St Vincent (where the mail boat starts), and returns from
Grenada or Trinidad. See Itinerary 3 for details.

Guesthouses

Caribbean travel can be *extremely* expensive. Rooms at typical
large resorts range from £60 ($100) to as much as £860 ($1500)
per day. This book avoids the tourist traps, concentrating on
guesthouses and small intimate inns; the more expensive hotels
we mention offer something special for the money. You may pay
as little as £6 ($10) per night for a guesthouse on the beach in
Barbados—or as much as £125 ($220) for a private island resort,
meals included, in the Grenadines. Most guesthouses range from
£17 to £30 ($30 to $50) per night for two people. Some include
meals.

Most Caribbean guesthouses are small family-owned operations with simple accommodation and good home cooking, island style. Lacking frills, they are usually much cheaper. As you'll spend the majority of your time out of doors, guesthouse accommodation will serve its purpose (a place to sleep) just about as well as expensive hotels—and you'll find the kind of West Indian hospitality most larger hotels don't offer.

Some guesthouses are like intimate B&Bs. West Indian style: renovated residences that may date back to pirate days, with four-poster beds and a Victorian or Georgian atmosphere. Others are very basic concrete block structures with two twin beds, a shared or private bathroom, fans, and a few books to help pass the time. Many offer cooking facilities, and you can usually eat with your hosts or at least get a cup of coffee in the morning.

Picky travellers may find that they don't have enough privacy, meal times are usually fixed, cockerels may crow at ungodly hours, pillows can be lumpy and the showers may even be cold.

But the positives far outweigh the negatives. Staying in guesthouses, you will set yourself apart from the invading hordes of tourists, find enriching new friendships and experiences, and bring home interesting travel tales. You'll get a firsthand look at the local food, customs and people. And you won't pay an arm and a leg for a room you use only to crash out in.

When you consider the advantages of guesthouses, you'll find that cold showers can be quite refreshing. Cockerels can be drugged (use a mixture of rice soaked in rum), or just use earplugs. Often your host will invite you to join in a family meal or event, and some will even take you sightseeing or picnicking if you chip in for the petrol. Personal attention comes from getting to know your host.

While we were touring the Caribbean to research this book, Cyndy caught a terrible cold. Our guesthouse 'mum' gave her a Vick rubdown and made her chicken soup. That's the kind of service you won't find at a big beach resort!

Transport

Your choice of island-hopping transport depends on two factors: time and comfort level. How much time do you want to spend in various airports waiting on delayed flights? Partying on a Windjammer or ferry en route between islands can be a lot more fun. You haven't totally experienced the Caribbean until you scoot across the crystal blue sea spotting islands as they pop up in the distance. On the other hand, some of your best photographic opportunities are aerial views of the islands you've visited, snapped just after your plane takes off. We prefer a combination of the two, making transport an interesting part of your holiday experience.

Caribbean island-hopping involves inter-island travel on local airlines and boats that may not even be listed on your travel agent's computer. Most West Indies public carriers are relatively small operations serving a limited number of islands. The novice island-hopper soon discovers that it can be virtually impossible to get from one island to the next without lengthy and expensive detours. For some islands, once you get there you can't leave until the next plane or boat comes by several days later. Each of the routes outlined in this book focuses on a selection of islands that offer not only maximum variety but also straightforward travel between destinations.

Inter-island ferries are found in the US and British Virgin Islands, St Kitts to Nevis, St Martin to Anguilla and St Barthelemy (known as St Barth, or St Bart's), Guadeloupe to Les Saintes, St Vincent through the Grenadines, and Carriacou to Grenada. Ferries are inexpensive and take from 20 minutes to two hours.

The Carib Islander, a picturesque old motor cargo boat, has been renovated into a fun cruise for approximately 60 people, meals included. It travels from St Lucia through the Grenadines, from the Grenadines to St Lucia, and from St Lucia to Martinique and back. Pick one trip or combine them all. They range from about £115 to about £260 ($200 to $450) — snorkel gear and meals included.

Windjammer cruises offers barefoot cruises on tall ships through the Bahamas, the British Virgin Islands, the Windward and Leeward Islands and the Grenadines. Most of the sailing is at night while you're sleeping, allowing maximum time on the islands and rocking you to sleep under the stars. One-week cruises cost £360 ($625) per person including meals. A 13-day cruise through the Grenadines, Antigua to Grenada and back, costs £760 ($1,325).

Charter boats are available for the cost of a luxury hotel (from £60 to £145 ($100 to $250) per person per day), food supplies included. To find charter companies, look for listings in special interest magazines. Day sails, available on many islands, usually include lunch and drinks. Some of the possibilities are described in this book's sections on individual islands. Check with your hotel for others.

By air: Most inter-island air passenger service is on small aircraft carrying from 4 to 44 passengers.

LIAT offers the most extensive island coverage, and several good packages are available for island-hopping. For example, the 'Super Caribbean Explorer Fare' gives you one month of unlimited island hopping in one direction, and a return trip to the originating island, for £210 ($365). The 'LIAT Explorer Fare' costs £85 ($149) for 21 days, including three stops and your return flight to the originating island.

Air BVI serves the US and British Virgin Islands, Anguilla, St Kitts and Nevis. **Windward Air** flies from St Martin to St Barth, Saba, Anguilla, St Eustatius, St Kitts and Nevis. **Mustique Airways** connects St Vincent and Mustique. **Air Martinique** flies between Martinique, Antigua, Barbados, Dominica, Grenada, Mustique, St Lucia, St Martin, St Vincent, Trinidad and Union Island. Other small inter-island air carriers are **Carib Aviation, Air Guadeloupe, Tropic Air** and **Montserrat Aviation.**

Travel agents

West Indies in Your Pocket is designed to help you avoid the conventional resort industry with its prepackaged '7 Days and 6 Nights in Fabulous Somewhere' trips. That doesn't mean you should shun travel agents. Some of our best friends are travel agents. A good, knowledgeable agent can save you time and long distance phone bills; he or she can probably find you bargains on airfare from home to your West Indies starting point; and best of all, the agent's services cost you nothing — his or her compensation is a commission on your airline ticket.

The only problem with most travel agents is information overload. While major resorts and package tour wholesalers have budgets that allow them to bombard agents with slick full-colour promotional literature, guesthouses and inter-island carriers do not. Most travel agents are not aware of bargains such as island-hopping through the Grenadines by mailboat for a few dollars, and can't tell you the ferry schedules connecting the Virgin Islands. Learning the personal side of any country's tourist scene requires years of research and on-the-spot experience.

But the travel agency business is changing fast. It's more competitive than ever before, and agents are discovering a whole new clientele: independent adventurers (that's you). Your local travel agent can build his or her Caribbean knowledge and contacts by helping you make arrangements for your tour, and may be eager for the opportunity. Ask, and shop around.

When you 'interview' a travel agent for the first time, be prepared to spend some time discussing your needs and desires, your travel budget, where you have travelled before and when, as well as such details as whether you drive an automatic car and whether you prefer a king size or two double beds. If the agent doesn't ask these questions, or doesn't respond knowledgeably to questions *you* ask, look elsewhere.

It's possible, I suppose, for an agent to know Caribbean leisure travel well even if he or she has never been there. Agents who want to specialise can attend seminars, classes, presentations and trade shows covering any region in the world, and many listen to feedback from clients returning from their trips. But if you ask an agent whether he or she has been to the Caribbean and the reply is, 'Just last year I went to the Bahamas', fake a yawn and move on.

Somewhere down the street may be a person who loves the West Indies, spends his or her spare time searching out little-known island destinations and special discount fares, dreams of the tropics nightly, and right now is hoping a client just like you will call.

Packing

Use soft luggage you can carry. You'll be spending quite a bit of time with it in airports. My favourite backpack has straps that zip out of sight making it look like real luggage. The old hippie hiker look doesn't get you far in the Caribbean, but shoulder straps come in handy at times.

Since humidity is always high in the islands, my best packing tip is to buy large waterproof zip-up bags (ship's chandlers may be an ideal source). Pack each item in one. Even a cotton skirt or trousers will fit. Sit on the bag to let the air out, stuffing loose edges as you go. While sitting on it, zip it shut.

This process vacuum seals your clothes, protecting them from dampness. They cannot wrinkle further, so if you iron them before putting them into the bags they'll look perfect upon removal. The end result is a pack or suitcase that closes more easily, full of neat, compact, moisture-proof little bags. When you need to rummage for something, simply dump the contents of your pack out on the bed, find what you're looking for and put the rest of the flat little bags back into the pack. It also protects your belongings if you get caught in the rain or splashed while riding a ferry. Take extra bags for wet flannels, suntan oil, seashells and such.

Bandanas: Carry several. Roll your money up inside one and tie it around your neck to carry it pickpocket-proof. It's more convenient than a money belt or hidden pocket in a tropical climate where clothing is minimal. Bandanas also double as flannels (which most guesthouses don't provide) and dry quickly.

Women: Be ruthless with yourself and *don't overpack!* In the West Indies more than almost anywhere, you can get by with practically nothing. Do take shorts and tops. (With a nice cotton skirt, jewellery, and maybe a shirt tied at the waist they make for ideal evening dress, and it's easier to carry extra tops for variety than extra skirts or dresses.) One pair of cotton trousers in a neutral colour — white or khaki — goes well with any colour. Roll up the trousers for sport, wear with heels for dressy occasions. Women can get away with anything in the islands, and you'll probably want to buy some new clothes en route anyway. Take a few small sample vials of perfume for perk-ups.

Men: If you want to visit a casino, go out for a nicer meal, or just in case you get invited for cocktails on someone's yacht, always carry a white cotton jacket and white cotton trousers: an instant suit that packs small. Sam has worn it in the best hob-nobby spots, with clean white deck shoes and a bandana tied around his neck — no problem.

Documents

Most islands require proof that you are who you say you are. A passport is always the best. While only necessary on some of the independent southern islands, a passport makes a good souvenir when filled with stamps from all the islands you've visited. Saba and Montserrat have the prettiest stamps.

Visas may be necessary. In the French islands you do not need a visa at this time. If they change the rule, you'll be able to get one upon arrival.

You'll go through a customs inspection upon arrival on every island except St Martin, Saba and St Eustatius. On these islands you simply breeze through, getting a validation on the immigration paper given to you on the plane. No baggage check.

Check with your travel agent or the various islands' tourist offices (see back of book) for current documentation requirements as these vary from time to time.

Other guidebooks

You won't need a comprehensive Caribbean guidebook to enjoy this trip. Write to the various island tourist agencies listed in the back of this book and they'll send you armloads of up-to-date, helpful information, including dates and details of festivals and other special events — it's free. Invest the money you save in a long novel to read during the lazy beach days.

Locally published guidebooks to individual islands are entertaining and occasionally indispensable. I've suggested some of the best in the appropriate sections of this book. They are sometimes available by mail order, but your best bet is to buy them as you arrive on the islands they cover.

Which trip for you?

In this book we describe three different trips and suggest possible variations on each one.

ITINERARY 1: The closer the islands are to the United States, the more commercialised and tourist-orientated they will seem. The first itinerary encompasses the **US Virgin Islands**, the **British Virgin Islands, St Martin** (Dutch and French), **St Barth** (French), **Anguilla** (British) and **Saba** (Dutch) — quite a variety of countries, all with gorgeous beaches, snorkelling, diving and sailing. There tends to be more nightlife, as well as good shopping buys (some duty-free).

ITINERARY 2: The second itinerary covers a range of islands with a less transient, more colonial feel, catering to a mix of American and European tourists. History buffs will find nautical history, old forts and beautiful Georgian renovations; nature lovers will discover rain forests, waterfalls, active volcanoes, caves, lush plantations, well-maintained gardens and flowers, and the last remaining Carib Indians. There are also plenty of great beaches and water activities. The itinerary encompasses **St Martin** (French and Dutch), **St Barth** (French), **Anguilla** (British), **Saba** (Dutch), **Antigua** (British), **Montserrat** and **Dominica** (both formerly British, now independent) and **Barbados** (also independent).

ITINERARY 3: The third itinerary, being the farthest away from the US mainland, is the most traditionally Caribbean. Transport may cost more, but inexpensive inter-island travel and accommodation will more than compensate for it. Because of the proximity to Venezuela and South America, you can experience a wide variety of ethnic foods, celebrations and foreign cultural influences. Once you go beyond Barbados and into the Grenadines, you won't see many big chain resort hotels. Cars are few, life is very West Indian. You'll end your trip in Trinidad, a melting pot of nationalities (35% of the population is East Indian). The itinerary includes the independent island nations of **Barbados, St Vincent and the Grenadines, Grenada** and **Trinidad and Tobago.**

ITINERARY 1

TOURS 1 – 3 Make your first stop **St Croix** in the US Virgin Islands for a gentle transition into 'island consciousness'. Check into a hotel in Christiansted and wander around the charming town. Rent a car the next day and visit Frederiksted on the other side of the island. On Tour 3, take an all-day side trip to nearby Buck Island for snorkelling or scuba diving.

TOUR 4 Catch the seaplane shuttle to **St Thomas**. After a day on the beach, take the ferry on to St John.

TOURS 5 – 7 Experience **St John**'s Virgin Islands National Park. Mix ranger-guided nature tours or self-guided walks with plenty of beach time. Relax.

TOURS 8 – 11 Make **Tortola** your home base for exploring the British Virgin Islands. Take the *Sundance II* ferry from St John to Tortola. Check into your hotel or campsite, and rent a car to spend the next two days seeing this island's best beaches and scenery, including Apple Bay, Carrot Bay, Cane Garden Bay, Brewer's Bay and Josiah's Bay. On Tour 11 take a day sail to **Virgin Gorda**.

TOURS 12 – 13 Fly from Tortola to **Anegada**, one of the best kept secrets in the Caribbean. Return to Tortola the next day.

TOURS 14 – 18 Fly to **St Martin**, where you'll experience two countries on one island: French St Martin and Dutch Sint Maarten. Enjoy the beaches (including an optional visit to a suits-optional beach) and the nightlife. On Tour 17 take a catamaran day sail to ritzy **St Barth**, and on Tour 18 ride the ferry to **Anguilla**.

TOURS 19 – 21 Fly from St Martin to **Saba**, 'The Unspoiled Queen', to sample Saba Spice, scale Mt Scenery and stroll around this delightful little Dutch island that is practically untouched by tourism.

TOURS 1 – 3

ST CROIX

This island is a good place to begin to get into an island frame of mind. The architecture has retained its delightful Danish qualities, with many of the old, 18th century, ballast brick buildings now transformed into boutiques and quaint courtyard cafes. The capital, Christiansted, is geared towards tourism with lots of activities and nightlife. Frederiksted, on the other side of the island, has a slower pace and a more local island feeling. Take your choice. The local quip is, 'You can go to Christiansted, or to Frederiksted, or to bed instead!'

Suggested schedule

Tour 1   Arrive in Tortola.
Check into your hotel.
Make arrangements for a hire car for Day 2.
If interested in a Buck Island trip, arrange day charter.
Dinner and club crawling in Christiansted.

Tour 2   Continental breakfast at your hotel.
Rent a car and head out towards Frederiksted.
En route, pick up lunch at Peter's Cellars (Sunny Isle Shopping Centre).
Picnic at the Botanical Gardens.
Visit the Cruzan Rum Factory.
See Whim Great House.
Tour around Frederiksted.
Return via the scenic drive or Mahogany Road and the rain forest.
Options: Spratt Hall Plantation for dinner; Jill's Stables for horse riding.

Tour 3   Take in the beaches, the east end of the island, or a side trip to Buck Island for snorkelling.
Laze around and enjoy the sunshine.

Catch the seaplane shuttle to St Thomas on Tour 4.

Getting there

Check with your travel agent for the best deal on airfares to St Croix. Apex fares booked three weeks in advance range from about £550 in winter to £600 in summer.

Getting around

Transport around the islands is by taxi or hire car. Driving is on the left in the Virgin Islands. Main roads are good; the most scenic roads are unpaved roads. Off season, you'll usually find cars available, but you may need a reservation in the winter.

Accommodation

Our favourite is the **Pink Fancy** on Prince Street, tel. 809-773-8460. Built in 1780, this small luxury hotel in downtown Christiansted offers large airy rooms that lack nothing (kitchen, TV, sitting area, current magazines and books, thick pink towels and great beds). The quiet Spanish courtyard invites you to the pool. The complimentary bar adds to a feeling that you are a temporary resident rather than just a guest. Mr Sam Dillon is the charming host who spent over a million dollars bringing this fine old hotel back up to scratch. Considering its accessibility to town, the complimentary continental breakfast and the 24-hour complimentary bar, the rates (winter, single and double £70-£85 ($120-$150); summer £35-£45 ($60-$75) depending on the size of the room) are a bargain. Call in advance in winter. There is a small grocery store on the same side of the street, for those wishing to cook for themselves. The seaplane shuttle is just down the road.

Three more good lodging choices are **The Lodge Hotel**, with friendly hospitality and budget rates (winter—single £25-£30 ($42-$50), double £27-£32 ($48-$55), continental breakfast included), located in the heart of town on Queen Cross Street, tel. 809-773-1535; and **Hill View Guest House**, tel. 809-773-1375/3542, in the centre of Christiansted, offering radio and kitchen privileges (winter: single £16 ($28), double £20 ($34); summer: single £13 ($22.50), double £16 ($28)); and **Ackie's Guest House**, tel. 809-773-3759, located in the hills; pool, kitchen privileges (single £17 ($30), double £23 ($40)). Other possibilities abound, including two Best Westerns and many resorts. You shouldn't have any problem arriving without a reservation, but it wouldn't hurt to make one for the first night just in case.

Food

Pentheny's, a National Historic Courtyard setting at 46 King Street, Christiansted, has good food and a lovely atmosphere.

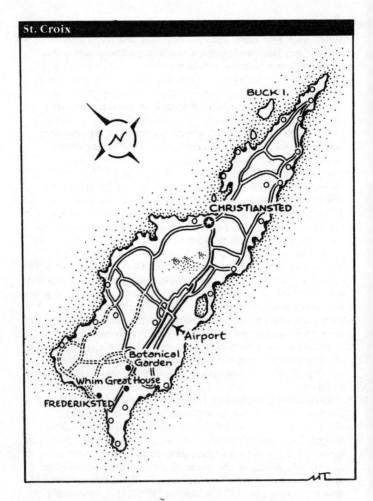

Owners Larry and Lisa use all fresh produce (local and imported), and the fresh fish is locally caught. The steps are lit with *luminaires* for a romantic atmosphere. Pianist on weekdays, jazz Fridays, Saturdays and Sundays.

Bombay Club, 5A King Street, is a fun place for dinner or appetizers. Try the rum cream pie that the bartender, Diane, makes. Jazz combo Wednesdays, Fridays and Saturdays, with Jimmy Hamilton (formerly of Duke Ellington's band). The Stone Pub is a fun spot.

Frank's, 1 Queen Cross Street, has Italian food, reasonable prices, good jazz, and chianti for 60p ($1). **The Luncheria** serves fast Mexican food and drinks in a courtyard setting across from Rumours. The burritos are huge for £1.50 ($2.50). At the **Kid Tough** café in Christiansted you can get local delicacies such as goat water and fungi. At **Roger's Place** on Company Street in Christiansted, the inexpensive specialities are local style food, seafood, and lobster.

New York Connection is a typical local snack bar and disco, serving items like fungi, callaloo, souse, chicken and plantain canoes stuffed with curried meat. It's on Highway (Hwy) 72 (Midland Road, near Bethlehem and Mt Pleasant). Edwin 'Eddie' Garcia, who manages the snack bar for his grandfather, makes a killer hot sauce that he swallows by the shot to entertain the tourists. Have a look at the art work in the disco; live band Friday and Saturday nights, £1.75 ($3) admission. To get there, turn right at McDonald's on Hwy 75, left at 707, right on Hwy 73, left on Hwy 72.

Villa Moralles, on Hwy 70, 5 miles before Frederiksted, serves pâtés, johnny cakes, plantain, paella (£10 ($17.50) for two); goat stew is the special on Thursdays and Saturdays. Open Thursday, Friday and Saturday, closed Sunday and Monday, lunch only Tuesday and Wednesday. The Villa also has a small (5-room) guest house, single £14 ($25), double £17 ($30).

Rita's Motown Bar, 60 King Street, Frederiksted, is an inexpensive local food spot and bar where you can meet the islanders. Try coconut water and gin.

Peter's Cellars, Sunny Isle Shopping Centre, offers 22 types of huge sandwiches, as well as gourmet items for making your own picnic, and a good selection of beers, wines and champagnes.

Night life
There are many pubs and courtyard cafés where you can enjoy an evening of jazz and conversation. Pick up a current copy of *St Croix This Week*, a very thorough guide to events around the island, at the airport or your hotel.

Sightseeing highlights
▲**Christiansted Walking Tour**—Get a map from the Visitors Bureau, in the Old Customs House in the centre near the park. The tour takes in a variety of 18th century buildings, with shopping and eating possibilities along the way.

▲**Saturday Market**—Local produce and fish are sold—a colourful sight.

▲**St Croix Botanical Gardens**—a former sugar plantation on Highway 70, gives tours, and has unique items in the gift shop.

Pick up a picnic lunch at Peter's Cellars (Sunny Isle Shopping Center) on the way.

▲**Cruzan Rum Factory**—Across from the Botanical Gardens, at Junction 70/64. Take a tour and taste.

▲**Whim Great House and Museum**—This historic plantation, originally built in the 18th century by a wealthy British merchant, has been renovated by the St Croix Landmarks Society. Period antiques are displayed. £1.75 ($3) for tour of house and grounds.

▲**Frederiksted Walking Tour**—Information at the Visitors Bureau, located in Frederiksted's Old Customs House, across from the pier.

▲**Spratt Hall Plantation**—On Hwy 63. Guided tours available, horse trails. The old plantation is a quaint (not to mention stuffy) hotel and a good place for dinner; reservations required, dress code.

Activities

▲**Buck Island**—Take a half- or all-day sail and snorkelling excursion to Buck Island Reef National Monument, with shallow marked trails perfect even for first-time snorkellers, guided expeditions and remote areas for expert divers. Charters are available on many local boats in Christiansted Harbour. Deep sea fishing charters are also available.

▲**Jill's Equestrian Stables** at Spratt Hall Plantation offers a pricey two-hour guided trail ride through the rain forest and up on a high ridge for a spectacular view.

▲**Windsurfing**—Lessons and rentals are available at Virgin Surf & Sail, tel. 773-4810, and at many of the resorts.

▲**Diving**—Scuba diving tours, lessons and equipment for hire are available at **Dive Experience**. They'll pick you up at your hotel. 24-hour booking, tel. 809-773-3307.

TOUR 4

ST THOMAS

Fly to St Thomas in the morning and spend the day there. Catch the afternoon ferry to St John. Though St Thomas isn't the best place for a relaxed vacation, you'll find enough of interest in Charlotte Amalie to keep you occupied for the day.

St Thomas is geared toward getting money out of the tourists. There are some good deals—gold, for example—but the atmosphere is one of hectic frenzy as cruise ship passengers descend en masse. From four to eleven boats at one time dock each day in Charlotte Amalie, the capital of the US Virgin Islands, making the town an intriguing spot for people watching and drooling over yachts in the harbour. It is also a good spot from which to depart on a charter boat bound for other, less hectic islands.

Suggested schedule

Morning	Take the seaplane shuttle to St Thomas.
Midday	Get your fill of duty-free shopping and cruiseship tourists, or take a taxi to Megan's Bay or Coki Beach for snorkelling.
Later	Take the ferry to St John. Check in at Cinamon Bay Campground, Maho Bay or other St John accommodation.

Getting to St Thomas

The departure tax from St Croix is £1.75 ($3). The Virgin Island Seaplane Shuttle will take you to St Thomas for £17 ($29) one way. Departures are once or twice per hour between 7:00 a.m. and 5:10 p.m. Call 809-773-1776, or toll free 800-524-2050. The seaplane shuttle is a unique flight: it takes off and lands in the water.

A new service between St Croix and St Thomas originates from **Hotel on the Cay**. The *VIP Commuter*, a 110-foot catamaran, makes the journey for £17 ($30) the round trip.

Getting around St Thomas

Taxis are not metered and official rates are listed in *St Thomas This Week* (copies can be found at the Seaplane Shuttle offices and around town). Most destinations can be reached for £1.75–£4 ($3–$7), depending on the distance.

Buses: Open-air buses leave Red Hook Dock hourly, from 7.15 a.m. to 6.15 p.m. They also leave the marketplace for Red Hook hourly, from 8.15 a.m. to 5.15 p.m. The cost is £1.20 ($2) each way. The Manassah Country Bus travels between Red Hook and town about every hour, starting at 6.05 a.m. from town and ending at 8.00 p.m. from Red Hook, costing 45p (75c). City buses go between Grand Union and the College of the Virgin Islands for 30p (50c). Other buses, about five per day, travel from the marketplace in town as far as West Bordeux for 45p (75c). Call 774-5678 for schedules.

Sightseeing shuttles: The shuttle to Coral World and Coki Beach leaves the Gray Line Tours office at the Grand Hotel in town at 9.30 a.m. and 12.30 p.m., returning at 1 p.m. and 3 p.m. (£2 ($3.50) each way, no service on Sundays). The shuttle to Jim Tillett Craft Studios leaves the Gray Line office daily at 9.30 a.m. and 12.30 p.m., returning at 1.10 p.m. and 3.10 p.m. (90p ($1.50) each way, no service on Sundays).

Accommodation

If you do decide to stay overnight, large hotels are expensive, so here are a few suggestions:

Bunker's Hill View Guest House, near the main street (tel. 809-774-8056) has air-conditioned guest rooms with kitchen, TV and complimentary breakfast (winter: single £22-£33 ($37-$55), double £27-£39 ($45-$65); summer: single £17-£27 ($30-$45), double £21-£27 ($35-$45). **Maison Greaux** overlooks the harbour, tel. 809-774-0063. Winter: single £20-£23 ($34-$38), double £26-£30 ($43-$50); summer: single £17 ($29), double £20-£24 ($34-$40). **Island View Guest House,** tel: 809-774-4270, has 9 rooms, most with private bath, and a restaurant and bar. Winter: single £27-£33 ($45-$55), double £30-£36 ($50-$60); summer: single £20-£24 ($33-$40), double £23-£27 ($38-$45). **Hotel 1829** is a city centre mansion inn with restaurant and bar (tel. 809-774-1829). All rooms have air conditioning, some have fans and some have cable TV. Winter: single £36 ($60), double £42 ($70); summer: single £27 ($45), double £33 ($55). Suites cost £60 ($100) or more. **Red Hook Mountain Apts.** (tel. 809-775-6111), close to the St John's ferry launch, rents studio apartments by the night for £48 ($80) (winter), £36 ($60) (summer), double occupancy. One and two bedroom apartments are also available. The apartments have a resident masseuse, pool, beach and tennis; watersports are nearby.

Food

Restaurants are everywhere! Our favourite is **Famous,** located in Frenchtown, serving local fish with unique and delicious sauces, as well as steamed vegetables and sushi (the real stuff). The decor is unpretentious, the meals are the best around and the prices are reasonable.

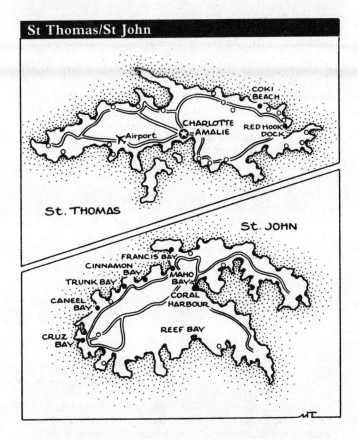

St Thomas/St John

Zorba the Greek, probably the only Greek restaurant in the islands, is on Government Hill next to Hotel 1829. Lunch costs £3.50-£6.00 ($6-$10). **Bill's Texas Pit Bar-B-Q,** a little harbourside stand in Red Hook, has £3 ($5) chicken, £4.20 ($7) short ribs, £4.80 ($8) beef brisket, or a £5 ($8.50) combination.

If you go to Jim Tillet Craft Studios, eat at **El Papagallo** where you'll get a good meal for under £6 ($10) and great frozen strawberry margaritas. **Windjammer** and **For the Birds** are fun places to try. **The Yacht Haven Bar** has 60p ($1) happy hour, as does **The Greenhouse.**

Getting to St John

The best, quickest and cheapest ferry is from Red Hook Dock, St Thomas to Cruz Bay Dock, St John, £1.20 ($2) one way for a 20-minute ride, leaving Red Hook at 6.30 and 7.30 a.m. (except weekends and holidays), and from 8.00 a.m. to 11.00 p.m. on the hour every day.

Between Charlotte Amalie, St Thomas (waterfront, near the Coast Guard Dock) and Cruz Bay, St John, the cost is £3 ($5) one way for a 45-minute trip. The ferry leaves every day at 9.00 a.m., 11.00 a.m., 3.00 p.m., 5.30 p.m. and 7.00 p.m.

Between Red Hook or Charlotte Amalie and Caneel Bay Plantation, St John, the cost is £5.50 ($9) from Red Hook, a 20-minute ride, departure 10.45 a.m., and £7 ($12) from Charlotte Amalie, a 45-minute ride, departures 9.45 a.m., 2.30 p.m. and 6.00 p.m. You can also go by water taxi, phone 775-6501 or 775-6972.

TOURS 5 – 7

ST JOHN

During the 1950s Laurence Rockefeller fell in love with St John and set out to buy up all the land he could to protect it from overdevelopment. After building Cinnamon Bay Campground and a luxury resort, Caneel Bay, he turned the remaining land over to the US government. The Virgin Islands National Park, dedicated in 1956, covers nearly two-thirds of the island of St John.

St John has grown a bit since the 50s, but it remains serene and natural. You'll find walking trails, beaches, old ruins to explore and unique camping facilities in private settings right on the water.

Suggested Schedule

Tours 5-7	Take your pick among the many National Park Tours activities. Mix in some beach time and let this be a relaxing part of your trip.

Getting around

Taxi rates from Cruz Bay range from 90p ($1.50) to Caneel Bay to £5 ($8) to Annaberg or Coral Bay, the most distant destinations on the island for one passenger, £1.75 to £6 ($3 to $10) for two. Two-hour island tours cost £11 ($18) for one or two passengers, £4 ($7) per person for 3 or more passengers. Pick up a St John information guide at your hotel for complete taxi rate listings.

Activities

▲**National Park Tours of St John**—Conducted by park rangers, reservations required, tel. 776-6201.

▲**Historic Bus Tour**—Mondays only—A special bus leaves the National Park Visitors Center, Cruz Bay, at 9.00 a.m. The tour last 3 hours and ends back at Cruz Bay. Cost £7 ($12).

▲**Reef Bay Hike**—Monday, Wednesday and Friday, £1.20 ($2)—The bus leaves the National Park Visitors Center for the trail at 9.45 a.m. Learn about tropical trees and plants, visit petroglyph carvings and an old sugar mill. A special boat takes you back to Cruz Bay by 3.30 p.m. for £3 ($5). Bring a lunch, drinks, and wear walking shoes.

▲**Salt Pond Hike**—Thursday, from 9.00 a.m. to 12.30 p.m. The bus leaves the National Park Visitors Center at 8.00 a.m. The cost is £6 ($10) for the round trip. The trail leads to Salt Pond and Trunk Bay. Bring lunch, a bathing suit and snorkelling gear.
▲**Advanced Snorkelling Safari**—Tuesday and Saturday, 2.00-4.00 p.m. Meet at Cinnamon Bay Lifeguard Station. Bring your mask, fins, snorkel and a T-shirt.
▲No reservations are required for: **Seashore Walk**—At 2.00 p.m. the ranger conducts a 1½ hour seashore tour, leaving from Annaberg Picnic Area. **Caneel Bay Walk**—Saturday, 10.00 a.m., historic tour. **Beginners Snorkel Safari**—Thursday and Sunday, 2.00-4.00 p.m., meet at Cinnamon Bay Lifeguard Station. Bring your mask, snorkel, fins and a T-shirt. **Bird Walk**—Tuesday from 8.30 a.m. to 10.30 a.m., from Francis Bay Warehouse. A taxi bus—cost £1.20 ($2)—leaves the National Park Visitors Center at 7.50 a.m.

Sightseeing highlights
▲**Annaberg Sugar Plantation** is an 18th-century renovation. Demonstrations of early plantation life (cooking, basketry, gardening, etc) are offered several times a week. There are also walking trails.
▲**Cruz Bay** boasts a variety of interesting shops, cafés and people. On Sundays there is always a party of some kind—reggae, jazz, an arts festival, etc. This is a good spot for getting picnic food and hiring a jeep.
▲**St John Museum,** a former great house, shows artifacts and gives information about the island's history.

Beaches
The most famous is **Trunk Bay,** where you can find an underwater snorkelling trail. Near Cruz Bay, it is a good swimming spot, but it can get crowded when the ships arrive at weekends. You'll find snorkelling equipment for hire, changing rooms, showers, a snack bar and a picnic area. Also popular is **Cinnamon Bay** in Virgin Islands National Park, with snorkelling and scuba gear for hire, changing rooms, showers and cafeteria.

Accommodation
Cinnamon Bay Campground has beachfront camping in a natural setting. Hire one of their fully-equipped platform tents or bring your own. There are also cottages. Activities include sailing, snorkelling, windsurfing, diving. Winter rates: £28 ($47) for 2 (tent), £6 ($10) for bare site, £34 ($56) for cottages. In the summer, tents are £22 ($37) and cottages £26 ($44). Tel. 809-776-6330.

Maho Bay Camp Resort has 96 beachfront cottages with all utensils and watersports. Walkways and platforms protect the environment. Commissary, restaurant. Summer £24 ($40), winter £36 ($60) for doubles. Tel. 809-776-6226.

Raintree Inn is located in Cruz Bay. Three 'efficiency' apartments with lofts rent for £39 ($65) in winter and £45 ($75) in summer. Guest rooms cost £27 ($45) and £30 ($50). Laundry. Tel. 809-776-7449.

Cruz Inn is right in town. Guest rooms with shared bath cost £30 ($50) in winter and £21 ($35) in summer, for 2. They also have efficiencies and 1-bedroom apartments. Tel. 809-776-7688.

Carla's Cottages, for 2 to 4 people, offers a little extra comfort. Regular rooms have a queen-size bed and bath for £66 ($110) during the winter and £46 ($77) during the summer. Apartments have a queen-size bed in a separate room, 2 day beds in the living room and a fully-equipped kitchen. Winter £100 ($165), summer £66 ($110). Cool pool and hot tub. Tel. 809-776-6133.

Food
Redbeard's Saloon, a favourite haunt on Coral Bay for the "yachtie" types, offers home-cooked meals. The adjoining boutique, Monkeyfist Studio, has some interesting items. Also in Coral Bay is **Shipwreck's Landing,** serving lunch and dinner from 10.00 a.m. to 10.00 p.m.

Raintree Terrace in Cinnamon Bay Campground has international cuisine and dining is al fresco.

For homely spots try **Fred's** bar, restaurant and cut-rate store. Fred's has West Indian food and surroundings, with a live band on Wednesdays and Saturdays. Also worth a visit is **Hercule's Pâté Delight,** open from 6.30 a.m. to 6.00 p.m. **Joe's Diner** in Cruz Bay is open from 7.00 a.m. to 6.00 p.m. for fast food, walk-up counter service. **Hazel's,** just past Coral Bay, is a worthwhile haunt, and Hazel herself is a real character. She runs the bar, cooks and tells good stories.

TOURS 8-10

TORTOLA

Tortola is the largest of the British Virgin Islands. Life there is
laid back. Visitors come to relax and enjoy the ultra-blue water
for sailing, snorkelling and diving. Surfers are drawn to 'hang ten'
and ride the big waves at Apple Bay and Carrot Bay, Tortola.
Private island resorts such as Peter Island, Mosquito Island and
Guana Island provide holiday spots for the rich and famous.

The British Virgin Islands are volcanic in origin except for
Anegada, a coral island. Tortola, the seat of British Virgin Islands
government, is the most populated, with 9,000 inhabitants. Virgin
Gorda has about 1,000 residents, while Jost Van Dyke and
Anegada each have between 100 to 150.

From Tortola, you can easily reach the other islands within the
British Virgin Islands by ferry or air shuttle.

Yacht charters are available for those with sailing skills. Crew
and captain can also be arranged for no more than the price for a
luxury room. £60-£90 ($100 – $150) per person per day includes
meals, diving equipment and accommodation on a 45-foot boat.
You can plan your island-hopping itinerary to include some of the
more expensive resort islands at ⅓ to ½ the price by sleeping
aboard the yacht. Windjammer Cruises offers a week-long sail
around the British Virgin Islands at less than £60 ($100) per day,
all inclusive.

Tortola's northern shore is where the white sand beaches are
found. The views are phenomenal, just what you came to see in
the Caribbean. Josiah's Bay and Little Bay boast calmer seas and
not many people. Our favourite, Brewer's Bay remains natural
and unspoiled, tree-lined, and has a great camp site.

The best surfing is in front of Sebastian's at Apple Bay, and in
Carrot Bay. Cane Garden Bay offers windsurfing, sunbathing and
hanging around at Rhymers Bar.

There are a few sights to see if you can get motivated enough
to leave the beach. We suggest you rent a car and spend at least
two days in Tortola. Some of the most enjoyable things to do are
visits to local spots for a beer, a conch fritter and conversation
with the island residents.

Getting there
Coming from St John, catch the *Sundance II* ferry at Cruz Bay
bound for Tortola, at 8:30 a.m. every day; 3:30 p.m. Monday to
Saturday; 4:30 p.m. on Sunday; and 5:00 p.m. Friday. £8 ($13)

each way. 25 minutes to West End Tortola. For further
information call 776-6282, 776-6141, 775-7408 or 776-6597.

Suggested Schedule	
Tour 8	Take the ferry from Cruz Bay, St John, to West End Tortola. Taxi to your hotel or directly to Budget Rental to hire a car. Check out the day sails to Virgin Gorda and make your reservation. Dinner at your hotel or in town.
Tour 9	Drive along the dramatic west coast to Apple Bay. The road gets steep and the view is worth many a picture. Continue to Carrot Bay and Cane Garden Bay for sunbathing and maybe surfing. Visit the Bomba Shack for lunch and a most authentic island experience. Dinner. Jules, in Carrot Bay, is the place for good local food.
Tour 10	Day cruise to Virgin Gorda on *Speedy's Fantasy* or *Speedy's Delight*.

A daily ferry service is also available direct from Charlotte
Amalie, St Thomas, on an open-air ferry, the *Bomba Charger* or
Native Sun. Current schedules are published in *St. Thomas This
Week* or the *British Virgin Islands Tourism Directory* available
from the BVI Tourist Board.

Getting around

Take a taxi to The Moorings for £3.60 ($6). Right around the
corner is Budget Rent-A-Car. Say hello to Mrs. Burke. Rhymers
in Cane Garden Bay also has cars for hire. Driving is on the left
side of the road. A local licence, available at the rental agency,
will be required and is valid for 3 months.

Bicycles are for hire in Roadtown at Hero's Bicycle Rental on
Main Street. Mopeds and tandems are also available.

Accommodation

Tortola has accommodation in all price ranges:
Brewer's Bay Campground charges only £10 ($16) for a
large tent with beds and lanterns, on a primitive white sand

beach. There are 20 prepared sites, as well as 15 bare sites for pitching your own tent (only £3 ($5)). They provide a bus service to town 3 times a day and will even fetch you some groceries if you can't pull yourself off the beach. They're busy in the winter season, not so full in the off season. There is a picturesque little beach bar that also serves food. Call 809-49-43463, or write to the owner's brother at PO Box 147, Cruz Bay, St John, USVI (postal service is much quicker to St John than to Tortola).

Tamarind Club is a hillside hotel and restaurant run by genuinely fun people. Located above Josiah's Bay; the rooms are simple but tastefully decorated; some have kitchenettes. No hot water, but a cold shower is rather pleasant after a hot day. There is a pool on the premises, as well as a bar and restaurant. The club has entertainment on weekends, and half of the island shows up to party. Tel 809-49-52477. Room rent is £24 ($40) in season; with kitchenettes £30 ($50).

Over the Hill Apts: £230 ($385) per week gets you a tastefully appointed apartment or cottage in a secluded part of the island by Little Bay, my favourite beach. If you want to do your own thing in peace and quiet, here's the spot. JC and his wife, the caretakers, are delighted people.

Rhymer's has rooms with kitchenettes, not fancy but clean. The cockerels get going at about three in the morning, so bring earplugs. £27 – £30 ($45 – $50) winter, £15 – £18 ($25 – $30) summer. Mr Rhymer has quite a monopoly on businesses: he runs the local car hire, watersports equipment hire, grocers, bar and restaurant. Tel. 809-49-54639.

Other suggestions: **Maria's by the Sea** walking distance to town, with hot plate, refrigerator, pool, restaurant; winter £36 – £50 ($60 – $80), summer £24 – £31 ($40 – $52); tel. 809-49-42771. **Village Cay,** winter £36 – £42 ($60 – $70), summer £27 – £33 ($45 – $55); air-conditioning, near downtown, 2 marina restaurants; tel. 809-49-42741. **Seaview Hotel**, winter £20 ($33), summer double £17 ($29); pool, cafe bar, hot water; tel. 809-49-42483.

Food
In Roadtown:
Midtown Restaurant is where all the locals eat breakfast and lunch. The decor is like a '50s American diner. Located on Main Street, they serve local dishes and sandwiches made with fresh ingredients. Good home cooking West Indian style. Also on Main Street is **Roti Palace.** With a name like this, it's worth a try.

The Wharf at Village Cay is a nice spot for dinner, featuring wahoo (a fish) cooked to perfection, a good selection of wines and real meat hamburgers. They'll prepare a local vegetable plate on

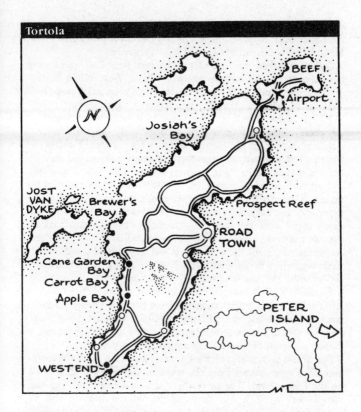

request.

Maria's, attached to the hotel with the same name, serves local food. Maria's soups are famous.

The Pub, on Marina Road (by Ft Burt), serves local fish such as wahoo and swordfish, as well as 'bangers' and chips. Every Wednesday night The Pub hosts a Trivial Pursuits competition with free champagne and shots of tequila to the winners.

Priscilla's restaurant serves real Mexican food (hard to find in the Caribbean). Her fajitas are outrageous, as is the empress taco with marinated steak. She also serves fresh fish, homemade pasta and, occasionally, duck. From nachos to a full dinner, prices are moderate from £5 to £6 ($8 to $10). It is also a fun night spot, drawing many locals when entertainment is featured.

Apple Bay/Carrot Bay/Cane Bay area:
Jule's at Carrot Bay is a place you can't overlook. It serves local food with a gourmet touch: shrimp, lobster, fish, conch plates,

johnny cakes, barbecue chicken and ribs. Jule's is an inexpensive, enjoyable place to have fun where you can meet people. Say hello for us. The conch fritters are the best anywhere.

Quitos has fish, steak, lobster and a nice wine list. The setting is a renovated sugar mill. **Sebastian's** has a West Indian buffet on Thursdays for £11 ($18.95), reservations required. **Coopers Friendly Club** in Carrot Bay is a typical local rum shop.

The Bomba Shack is about the wildest place we've found anywhere in the Caribbean. The decor is 'early junkyard'. Artifacts include an old blender hanging from a tree, T-shirts from surfers who sipped brew there in times past, an old stop light, a broken phone hanging from another tree, lots of grafitti and artwork added randomly on the walls. Bomba exemplifies the saying, 'One man's trash is another man's treasure'. You must experience his hospitality and charm to understand. His little shack opens when the surf's up, catering to beach bums from all over and offering a good cheap meal (cooked in an old tyre rim converted to a grill). Bomba serves goat, chicken ribs and local fresh vegetables for around £4 ($7) for the first plate, £1.75 ($3) for seconds. He's an interesting conversationalist.

Scatliffe's. Full course dinner featuring native dishes. Afterwards, you'll be entertained by the Scatliffe family fungi band. It's like being invited home for Sunday dinner. Hours are 7:00-10:30 p.m., reservations required (there are only 6 tables); Lunch is served between 11:30 a.m. and 2:00 p.m.

For drinks at sunset, there's a tremendous view of the British and US Virgin Islands from the mountaintop **Skyworld,** located on the Ridge Road. The drive there is a bit treacherous, but the view is well worth it. I recommend the soursop daiquiris and conch fritters. They also serve a 6-course meal or a la carte.

Church ladies dinner: On Fridays at the Ballfield, the local church ladies have a chicken and fish fry. Everyone turns out for an evening of music. Dinner costs £2.25 ($4).

Sightseeing highlights
▲**The Botanic Gardens** are well maintained and worth seeing if you are interested in fauna and flora. Located near the recreation ground in Roadtown.

▲**Callwood Rum Distillery** has been a local family business for over 200 years. Makers of Arundell rum, they are located in Cane Garden Bay. No phone, just stop by for a visit and see how rum is made — with equipment similar to old-fashioned moonshine stills.

Activities
▲**Underwater exploration.** Some of the best sightseeing is

done under the sea. Snorkelling and diving trips to the wreck of the *Rhone* or to the many coral reefs can be arranged through Underwater Safaris, tel. 809-49-43235, at the Moorings Dock, or through Aquatic Centers, tel. 809-49-42858/9 (toll-free, 800-345-6296), at the Treasure Isle Hotel and Prospect Reef. See *Welcome* Magazine for other listings.

▲**Island Diver,** tel. 809-49-43878, in Village Cay Marina, has all-day excursions. Barbecue on a 65-foot boat, from £45 ($75).

▲**Offshore Sailing School:** Learn to sail. A week-long course costs £325 ($545), and a bare boat preparation course is £340 ($575). Classes start on Sundays. Contact the Offshore Sailing School, East Schofield Street, City Island, New York 10464, USA, for details.

▲**Windsurfing School** guarantees to teach you how. The school is located at Trellis Bay on Beef Island. Free pick-up and delivery. Advanced and beginner. Tel. 49-52447 or write to Boardsailing, Box 537, Long Hook, Tortola.

▲**Day sails.** Look up our cousin Dick Azzolina for day sails or information about the island's activities. You can contact him through The Moorings; he is on the boat called *How Sweet It Is.* Be prepared for laughs. If you're a single woman, be prepared.

Helpful hints

Launderettes: There are several in Tortola. If you need anything washed, do it here — they are not as convenient elsewhere. At the foot of Zion Hill is a laundry that washes and folds for £3.50 ($6) a bag, any size. Rhymer's at Cane Garden Bay also offers wash-and-fold service, or you can wash it yourself.

Photographs: Kis Photo has a 1-day service if you can't wait until you get home. They process prints and Ektachrome slides and are located upstairs in the Venterpol Bldg. Say hello to our friend Lena Penn. It is a good place to contact Dick Azzolina for day sails on *How Sweet It Is.*

Massage: For a nice bit of extravagance, visit the Massage and Body Work Clinic at the Prospect Reef Resort and Peter Island Hotel.

TOUR 11

DAY TRIP TO VIRGIN GORDA

Virgin Gorda is a popular yacht stop. The Baths' caves and
unique rock formations are the attraction. This is a perfect place
to sun and snorkel for at least a day. The beach itself is small.
Pools are created by the large granite boulders. Spring Bay,
Devils Bay and Trunk Bay are popular beaches.

Suggested schedule

Morning	Ferry from Tortola to Virgin Gorda. Taxi to The Baths. After exploring the sea caves, spend the day snorkelling or lying on the beach in the vicinity of The Baths, or try one of the other beaches, of which there are 20 on the island.
Evening	Ferry back to Tortola

Getting there
The ferry leaves from Tortola on Monday, Wednesday, Friday
and Saturday, returning the same day. On Sundays there are two
boats to and from Virgin Gorda, *Speedy's Fantasy* and *Speedy's
Delight*.

   If you choose to spend any night but Friday or Saturday here,
you'll be stranded on the island for a second night due to the
ferry schedule.

Getting around
You can take a taxi to The Baths, Savanna Bay, Spring Bay, or
Devils Bay for about £2.25 ($4) the round trip from the dock.
You can also rent a moped from Harrigan Rent-A-Cycle, at the
Village Gorda yacht harbour. Phone ahead on Sundays,
809-49-55542.

Water sports
Dive BVI offers scuba diving tours and rental. Tel. 809-48-55513.
It is located at the Virgin Gorda yacht harbour. Kilbride's Underwater Tours in North Sound offers scuba and snorkelling, tel.
809-49-42746.

Food

Try **The Big Yard** on the way to The Baths. The bar is open daily from 11:00 a.m. until midnight. Lunch and dinner are served, and a local scratch band entertains on Saturdays.

The Bath and Turtle has sandwiches, hamburgers, steak and lobster in a pub-like atmosphere. It is located at the Yacht Harbour Shopping Center.

The Wheelhouse, by the Ocean View Hotel serves native dishes and seafood. Lunch from £1.50 ($2.50), dinner from £3.50 ($6). Informal.

Accommodation

If you wish to stay overnight in Virgin Gorda, try **The Ocean View Hotel,** tel. 809-49-55230. The rates are £36–£42 ($60-$70) (winter) or £27–£30 ($45–$50) (summer); or **Guavaberry Spring Bay,** where you can get a 1-bedroom house for £57 ($95) in winter, £39 ($65) in summer, or a 2-bedroom house for £90 ($145) winter, £55 ($93) summer. Tel. 809-49-55227. Kitchenettes, commissary, beach.

TOURS 12 – 13

ANEGADA

Anegada, among the best kept secrets in the Caribbean, is my favourite hideaway. Locals from neighbouring islands tried to scare us from going there with tales of man-eating sharks that literally come out of the water to get you and scorpions the size of your fist. We only found fabulous beaches where you can walk for miles and miles, and a small population of very friendly people. Over 100 known wrecks lie off the coast by Horseshoe Reef, and rumour has it that there may be a total of 250 wrecks — surely a diver's paradise. The island is totally flat.

Suggested schedule

Tour 12	Fly to Anegada. Check into Soares Campground or Reef Hotel. Laze around on the beach or go diving.
Tour 13	Fly back to Tortola. Either continue to St Martin or spend the night on Tortola and go on to St Martin the following morning.

Getting there

From Tortola, take Air BVI (Mondays, Wednesdays, Fridays and Sundays, 7:00 a.m., 12:00 noon and 5:00 p.m.). It's about a 15-minute flight.

Biras Creek, a luxury hotel on Virgin Gorda, sometimes offers ferry excursions to Anegada. Check with them for times. Tel. 809-49-43555 or 43556.

Food and lodging

The Reefs Hotel, offers 12 rooms on half board. Diving is available there. Tel. 809-49-43425; ask the Marine Operator for Anegada Reef. Or write to Lowell Wheatley, Reefs Hotel, Anegada BVI and allow plenty of time for a response.

The other lodging choice is to stay with our friends, Vernon and Julie Soares, at **Neptune's Treasure.** They are in the fishing business, but they also have a few tents to rent for £6 ($10) per person, each with a mattress and sheets: quite cosy accommodation. If you bring your own tent, the cost is £1.20

($2), but cooking is discouraged. They have an excellent restaurant and bar, inexpensive, serving fresh fish, lobster and home-cooked meals. If you eat what the family is eating for dinner, the cost is considerably less. The only way to contact them is by radio on VHF Channel 16.

On Loblolly Bay, you'll find a snack bar offering lobster and local vegetables as well as mixed drinks.

Wilfred, the taxi driver, has recently built a bar and restaurant about a mile from Neptune's Treasure. He did a beautiful job designing this structure, and it is enhanced by its open atmosphere looking out on a pristine white sand beach. If you start walking from Neptune's Treasure, more then likely Wilfred will chance by and give you a lift. From his place you can walk for miles and see no one. The area is a great picnic spot, too.

Sightseeing
There are no sightseeing highlights on Anegada. Just explore the island coves and beaches. Meet the people. Your stay on Anegada will be one of the most relaxing parts of your Caribbean trip.

Return to Tortola
The same flights that go to Anegada (see 'Getting there') turn right around and go back to Tortola. Check the times when you purchase your round-trip tickets, then reconfirm on arrival in Anegada.

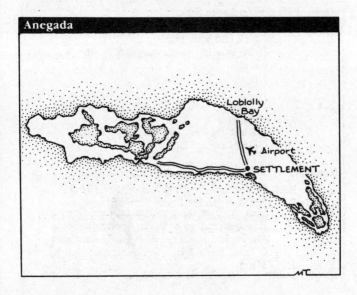

TOURS 14-16

FRENCH ST MARTIN/
DUTCH SINT MAARTEN

You get two countries for the price of one on this stop. The Dutch side, Sint Maarten, and French side, Saint Martin, are only divided by a commemorative marker to acknowledge your passing from one country to the other.

There is something for everybody here. The wide choice of restaurants includes some of the world's best, and eating is almost a sport. You can play tourist at the casinos and shop duty-free in Phillipsburg. Or adopt the beach bum approach and simply laze around on the beach with a loaf of bread, a jug of wine (cheap and great) and some authentic Dutch gouda cheese, an ever popular pastime on the island.

Suggested schedule

Tour 14   Arrive from Tortola.
Before you leave the airport, buy your round-trip ticket to Saba.
Hire a car from Speedy Rent-A-Car.
Check into your hotel.
Drive around and get acquainted with the island.
Dinner in Phillipsburg.

Tour 15   Beach time at Club Orient or, if you're shy, elsewhere.
Marigot for shopping and happy hour.
Grand Case for dinner.

Tour 16   Beachcombing, windsurfing, snorkelling, shopping or whatever you feel like doing—maybe a day sail to Tintamere.
Visit the time share apartments for a free catamaran trip to St Barth, or stop by Bobby's Marina and buy a ticket. If you're not flying to Saba, buy a boat ticket to get there on the *MV Style*.

Getting there

Fly LIAT or BWIA to St Martin. Arrival is at Queen Juliana Airport, on the Dutch side. No customs. All you'll encounter is a brief pause to turn in the immigration paper you received on the plane and get your passport stamped. If you've packed light and carried everything on you, you won't have to wait amongst the incredible mass of tourists for your luggage to show up.

Transport

You must hire a car to get about, since taxis are expensive (at least £8 ($13) between the French and Dutch side). For mobility and a good deal (£20 ($35) and up per day) go to Speedy's at the airport.

Driving is on the **right** side and you can go from one end of the island to the other in less than 20 minutes.

St Barth, Anguilla and Saba are close enough for 1- or 2-day side-trips. Or try sailing on one of the day-sail trips to Tintamere, an uninhabited private island approachable only by boat. It's a good party for the day.

Activities

Life here is truly a beach, and St Martin has some of the best. Our favourite is **Club Orient,** on St Martin (French side), a lovely nudist resort. (If you are shy about shedding your clothes, leave them on. Sniggering is frowned upon at suit-optional beaches. So are cameras!) Whenever we feel the troubles of the world 'bare-ing' down on us, or a cold wave approaching, 'Club O' is the place we head for. It is a Caribbean utopia, offering the weary soul refuge and a chance to let it all hang out in the best sense of the word.

▲**Beachcombing** along one of the many beaches and coves, some of them accessible only by boat, can make for an enjoyable day. Take a picnic. Your hotel will pack a box lunch for you, or **Eat Royal** in Phillipsburg makes a gourmet basket; you can also stop in the **Food Center** (Dutch side, on the road to the airport) to buy your own ingredients. Charter a sunfish or sailboat for a more private excursion.

▲**Watersports:** windsurfing, snorkelling, sunfishes and deep-sea fishing are a few of the ocean-related sports you'll find in St Martin. Your hotel or guest house can steer you toward watersports; try the folks at Club Orient or Le Galion on the French side. Maho Reef also has a large watersports area—but it's a large resort, too.

▲The best **shopping** is in the duty-free port of Phillipsburg. There you can find inexpensive perfume, jewellery (though we've done better at Christmas sales at home), ghetto blasters and other electronic equipment (hope it works when you leave), china and crystal. Again, we'd rather hit a sale back home than drag china around the Caribbean. If you feel like hauling booze around (though it never seems worth its weight in your backpack or suitcase) it's cheaper here.

▲Phillipsburg's best deals on clothing are at **New Amsterdam** and **Around the Bend.** Dutch appliqué work on tablecloths and napkins is a good buy.

▲Marigot is the place for fun, kinky French cotton clothes. The prices can be rather high, but watch for sale items. Naf Naf, a popular brand, has reasonably-priced fun styles.

▲Casino chips, dinners for two and trips to St Barth or Saba are among the incentives that lure travellers to spend an hour prowling through the time-share apartments. Some car hire agencies offer £30 ($50) discounts if you visit a time-share . . . not bad for an hour's time.

▲**Bobby's Marina** is a good people-watching spot. Yachts from all over the world pull up, and a fun crowd gathers at the bars at sundown.

▲**Day Sail to Tintamere:** The *Tri'n Sea* is the best choice for a long sail and excellent cuisine. Stewart, the captain, is also the chef, and his passengers rave about his culinary ability—usually a barbecued swordfish or chicken with lots of tasty salad, prepared on the boat upon arrival at the private island of Tintamere. Drinks are included as well, and high tea is served as you sail around the bend to Great Bay Marina in the afternoon. Tickets can be purchased from Chesterfields or through your hotel. They're also offered as time-share apartment freebies.

▲For a trimaran experience in the buff, sail on the *Sygried,* which leaves twice weekly from Club Orient to Tintamere. Peter Wipp is your captain and host. Drinks are included as well as a luncheon buffet of salads, pâté, sliced meats, fruits and cheese—all attractively presented on palm fans. Clothes are optional and cries of mutiny are often heard as Peter begins to sail back at the end of the day. £30 ($50) for a round trip. This can be a serious party with the right crew—and mean serious burns: bring suntan oil.

Food

French side:

The best bargain on the island, in my book, is **Pedro's** beach shack on Orient Beach. Pedro serves fresh barbecue chicken for £3 ($5), ribs for £3.50 ($6) and swordfish for £4 ($7). Meals come with fresh french fries and/or salad. Mix the barbecue sauce with the yellow West Indian pepper sauce . . . He sells cold drinks and booze. He is at the far end of the beach, not on Club Orient property.

Papagallo, the restaurant at Club Orient, used to be good, and if cook Angelique is still there it should be now. Her linguine and the steak au poivre are worth trying.

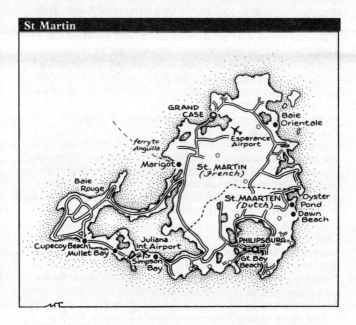

Local food is a speciality at **Yvette's,** about half a mile before Club Orient. She piles on the food and gets rave reviews.

Mark's Place, an informal lunch and dinner spot popular with the Club Orient crowd, has a good selection of beers and wines. It's located past Club Orient, at Cul-de-Sac, down a road so rough you'll be glad you're driving a hire car instead of your own.

Breakfast at **Mastadona** is the best deal in Marigot. They put a basket of wonderful pastries, warm from the oven, on your table and charge you only for the ones you eat. Good omelettes too. The Canadian owner is a delightful man who will sit and talk with you, if he has time, and help you figure out the area.

Le Jardin in Marigot serves a filling, budget-priced fish soup chock full of lobster, crab and fish chunks. Also, sandwiches and light meals.

Le Bistro Nu in Marigot serves inexpensive local cuisine, good and filling.

You can get a great barbecue chicken dinner late at night at the **Walt Disney Snack Wagon,** in Marigot by the school.

Of course, you must try our good friends at **Bertine's** in La Savana for French cuisine and Chicago-style ribs. Chris and Bernie will do everything they can to see that you enjoy the evening. The food and wine, and their personal attention, make the place a memorable experience.

There is a variety of great little cafés around La Marine Port Royal. You can get a pizza for 40 francs (about £4 ($7)), or a plate of linguine. **Café de Paris** is a good spot for happy hour and people watching. Cyndy's still trying to figure out how the local French women stay so skinny. Café de Paris has good food and jazz many nights.

Chez Martine, in Grand Case, specialises in French food and desserts that are almost obscene.

Another great French spot is **Neptune,** with our friend Joel. Say hello. The dining room overlooks the ocean and piano music is featured; a great wine selection, champagne. It's hard to suggest other restaurants in Grand Case because there are so many—generally romantic and expensive—and owners change frequently. Wander about looking at the menus before you choose one.

Dutch side:
Located at Pointe Blanche, **Zachary's** has the best ribs I've eaten in a long time. Taste the key lime pie!

Sam's Place is where the locals and 'yachties' hang out for happy hour or a good breakfast, lunch or dinner. It is located by Bobby's Marina, at the end of Front Street, in Phillipsburg.

The West Indian Tavern is typically Antillian. It offers gingerbread and has colourful decoration. Take home a bottle of Guavaberry liqueur.

For lunch, you can get the best hamburger at **Callaloo** and great sandwiches too. Flying fish creole is an excellent choice for dinner. Their pizzas used to be great but now are only fair. This is a popular happy hour spot. Also try the restaurant at the **Airport Lounge.**

Eat Royal is a chic place for lunch and offers picnic boxes to take away if you call ahead. Here you can pick up pâtés, cheeses, pastries, breads and salads along with a nice bottle of wine. Located on Front Street, this was the site chosen for Queen Beatrix's lunch on her last visit to the island.

Greenstreets has 60p ($1) happy hour with hors d'oeuvres from 4.00 to 6.00 p.m. Their menu is of the fern-bar type.

Paradise Café offers mesquite-grilled fish and chicken, Mexican food and fabulous linguine. Say hello to Dominique and Byron, and buy them a drink for us. A fun crowd frequents here, and a swimming pool is available for the use of the patrons. To get there, turn on a small dirt road by Studio 7. Also visit their other restaurant, **Pinocchio's** in Phillipsburg, featuring pasta, Italian specialities and a good bar overlooking the ocean.

Dominique's brother owns **Escargot,** featuring nice appetisers and full French meals. For a culinary splash out, eat at **Le Bec Fin.** They are masters of presentation and the food melts on your tongue.

Accommodation

French side:
Club Orient is a fun place to stay. Their chalets have queen-size beds, fully-equipped kitchens, private baths, plus an outdoor sunshower on the back porch. You can get one efficiency size room or a house with separate bedroom, living room and kitchen. Some are right on the beach. If you cook some of your meals and mix your own cocktails, you can make staying here a bargain. You'll meet so many nice people you won't feel like leaving . . . but some of the old regulars are being driven away by price increases and choose to stay in other accommodation, using the beach by day. There is an enjoyable restaurant and bar on the premises, a boutique and small grocery. Prices: studio, winter £70-£105 ($120-$173), summer £43-£58 ($72-$96); chalet garden, winter £125-£170 ($210-$285), summer £70-£90 ($120-$152). Contact Club Orient, tel. 590-873-3385 (toll-free 800-828-9356). Except during the high season, there are usually one or two rooms available if you just happen to drop by.

Bertine's, at the top of the hill in La Savana, is a cosy spot with 5 rooms (double beds) in a homely atmosphere. Rooms, each with private bath, are inexpensive and comfortable. Chris and Bernie Poticha have a French restaurant on the premises. Ask them about entertainment on the island, maybe they'll join you after the restaurant closes. They also own property on the island of Saba and can tell you anything you want to know. Prices: £35-£45 ($55-$75).

Palm Plaza is a small hotel with attractive, clean suites, interestingly designed. 20 regular rooms cost £28 ($46), suites £36 ($60), suites with kitchen £42 ($70). Located in the centre of Marigot, near cafés, bars and the harbour. The manager is Alain Fiston. Tel. 596-875196; address: Rue de la Republique, 97150.

Hostellerie l'Ermitage has 10 simply-furnished rooms with private showers and balcony. Single £21-£24 ($35-$40), double £27-£30 ($45-$50), winter; summer £19 ($32) and £22 ($37). The manager is George Lake. Tel. 596-875033; address: Rue de la Liberté, 97150.

Dutch side:
The **Passangran** has a most charming atmosphere. Formerly the
official government guest house and one of the oldest on the
island, it is located on Front Street in the heart of Phillipsburg.
The beachside veranda is a nice place to meet for afternoon
cocktails or complimentary tea and biscuits. The food at the hotel
is not impressive, but the ambiance makes up for it. Sam's Place
is nearby for breakfast and lunch. Winter rates are £47, £53, £62
($79, $88, $103); summer £32 ($54) and £38 ($64). Address:
Great Bay Beach, PO Box 151, Phillipsburg; tel. (011-599-4)
23588.

   Chesterfields is recommended if you want to be near Bobby's
Marina for a day sail. There is a risk of crime in the port
vicinity, so make sure your belongings are safe.

   Rama Apartments are very reasonable—winter £27-£36
($45-$60), summer £15-£21 ($25-$35). Located at Point Blanch,
near Zachary's Ribs, Rama has 16 rooms with air-conditioning, a
pool, a grocery shop on the premises, and car hire. It is run by a
delightful East Indian family; mum is Betsey Ramdas. Tel.
(011-599-4) 22582; address: Box 227, Phillipsburg.

   Oyster Pond is my favourite for casual elegance. It is
expensive, but what a nice touch of class! The setting and decor
are very Caribbean, with wicker and cool fabrics. If you choose to
stay elsewhere, at least come by for a look and a drink by the
ocean. Tel. (011-599-4) 22206/23206; address: Box 239,
Phillipsburg. Winter from £160 ($270), summer from £95 ($160).

Nightlife
The best nightlife is on the Dutch side because that's where the
casinos are.

   Studio 7 is open from 11.00 p.m. to 7.00 a.m. for those night
owls who like disco music and a really 'in' crowd. Located across
from Maho Reef.

   Another favourite late night haunt is **The Jolly Roger Bar.**
Sometimes they pass out instruments to the drinking public and
rouse enthusiastic audience participation in the evening's
entertainment. If you want to meet someone, there's nothing like
playing a washboard to make it happen. Jolly Roger is open from
10.00 p.m. to 6.00 a.m. You can get barbecue chicken with
potato salad, and beans for £4 ($7) late at night only. If you
forget to find a room, this is a good place to pass the night.

   The bigger resorts and time-share apartments offer
entertainment. Check *St Martin Holiday* or *What's Happening St
Martin* for current information.

   On the French side, **Club Orient** has entertainment (jazz or
reggae) on Thursday nights and Sunday afternoons. **La**

Habitacion has a great disco in a unique setting. Something is always happening around the marina in Marigot.

Helpful hints

There are two things that don't work in French St Martin, the phone and the gendarmes. If you can avoid it, don't use either, it's a frustrating experience.

Even telephoning from the French side to the Dutch side is practically impossible. We were told that all calls go through Guadeloupe—and sometimes Paris—even though Phillipsburg is just a few miles away. The system was revamped recently but didn't improve. Telephone service is much better in Phillipsburg (Dutch side). You can make phone calls from your hotel, or go to the Lands Radio by the Pondfill.

Hats off to the French Tourist Board who helped intercede with the gendarmes when our hire car was stolen. The police wouldn't take our report or offer assistance; and, worst of all on a tourist resort island, they didn't speak any English. The Tourist Board, located by the harbour in Marigot, was most helpful. (Apparently, someone just needed wheels to get to the disco; our car showed up the next day.)

Camping is possible on Tintamere or Green Key, both across the bay from Club Orient. You can hire a dinghy at Robert's Seashell Stand, near Pedro's at Orient Beach, to get you to the island. Some people pitch a tent anywhere that looks secluded, but we would suggest asking first if camping near a hotel.

TOUR 17

DAY TRIP: ST BARTH

St Barthelemy (commonly called 'St Barth' or 'St Bart's) is a small, quiet island without big hotels, casinos or nightclubs. It is a beautiful spot — and very expensive, which is why we suggest you visit for the day instead of staying overnight

The trick on this island is to avoid spending too much money. A good time on St Barth can put the average person in the poorhouse. A friend tells us she recently paid £6.50 ($11) for two beers and an ice cream cone at the airport snack bar; lunch for two can easily cost £30 ($50) if you're not careful. But there is a way around this problem: stick to the 'loaf of bread, jug of wine, and Thou' theory. Good French wines are inexpensive, and so are French bread, croissants and cheese. You can buy fresh fruit at the open markets on Thursday and Friday, although you should negotiate the price since fruit is also expensive (usually imported). If you must eat a real meal, do so at snack stands on the beach where fresh fish is often the fare. Always ask the price first.

You'll find some great jazz clubs in St Jean. You may feel like splashing out on a drink or two here. The beaches are free (the best things in life usually are). Snorkelling is good at Baie St Jean. The water is calm and perfect for windsurfing. Monokinis (topless) are the norm, and nude sunbathing, although illegal, goes on anyway at some beaches.

Suggested schedule

9:00 a.m.	Leave Bobby's Marina on a catamaran bound for St Barth.
	Visit Gustavia, the island's main town, then head up the coast to the fishing village of Corossol.
	Spend the afternoon on Baie des Flammands, a beautiful, uncrowded beach, or on the other side of the island at Baie St Jean, the heart of the island's exclusive resort scene.
Evening	Return to St Martin.

Getting there

Your best bet is a day sail on a catamaran such as the *Maho* or

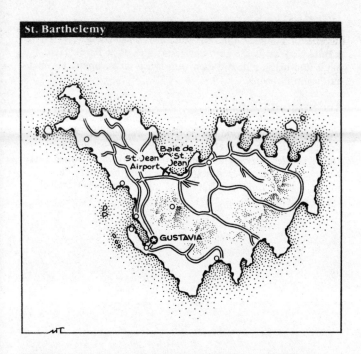

The Eagle from Bobby's Marina, St Martin. You can sail round
trip for £30 ($50), including drinks. Depart from Bobby's Marina
at about 9:00 a.m., return around 5:00 p.m. Buy tickets the day
before, or visit a time-share apartment and get your tickets free.

Windward Air also has flights several times a day for £24 ($40)
round trip. The approach to St Barth is a trip in itself.

You can hire a car on St Barth for £24 ($40) (24 hours).

Sightseeing highlights

▲**Gustavia,** St Barth's capital, has a busy port with plenty of
shopping opportunities. The market is held on Tuesdays and
Thursdays at the foot of Rue de la France. Notice that many
signs in Gustavia are bilingual — French and Swedish. For over a
century, this island was Sweden's only colony in the New World.

▲**Corossol** is a very traditional French colonial fishing village.
Clothing styles haven't changed much since the 17th century, and
the local residents speak an Old Norman French dialect. Straw
weaving is the local craft. The village is about three miles
northwest of Gustavia.

▲**Baie des Flammands** is an uncrowded beach on the north
shore, about three miles by road past Corossol. From the beach,

an easy walking trail winds to the top of the volcano that made
this island. The view from the summit is outstanding.
▲**Baie St Jean** is the glittering resort area of St Barth. Here
you'll find half a mile of beach with lavish villas, up-market shops
and beautiful people.

Accommodation.

I suggest St Barth as a day trip because accommodation can be
very expensive. If you do decide to stay overnight or longer,
Village Saint-Jean Hotel has double rooms for £50 ($84),
studios (garden, terrace) for £56 – £70 ($94 – $118) at winter rates.
Water sports, kitchen facilities, 2 miles from the beach; on a
hilltop, 1 miles from the airport, 1½ miles from Gustavia. Tel.
596-276-139.

TOUR 18

DAY TRIP: ANGUILLA

These are the beaches you see in travel posters: transparent blue seas and white — *really* white sand beaches. You can reach Anguilla in 15 minutes from Marigot Harbour in St Martin. Pick up a bottle of wine, some cheese and fruit for a delightful picnic, or stop in one of the restaurants at Road Bay or Shoal Bay.

Suggested schedule

Morning	Ferry from St Martin to Anguilla.
	Taxi or take a tour to Shoal Bay and lie in the sun for the day;
	Or, hire a moped and explore the length of this narrow island.

Getting there

The ferries from St Martin (Marigot Bay) cost £3 ($5) each way and run every hour or two, from 8:00 a.m. to 5:00 p.m. Schedules are posted by the pier, and printed on little cards found everywhere. The trip takes about 15 minutes.

A tour costs £24 ($40) round trip to Shoal Bay, the most popular beach.

A car or moped will allow you to scoot about the island. Bennies Tours Car Rental is about ½ mile from the port.

Sightseeing

Aside from two ponds near Road Bay where salt is harvested from the sea, Anguilla has no real sightseeing attractions. Instead, you'll find almost fifty miles of the world's most beautiful beaches.

Accommodation

If you opt to visit overnight, stay at **Rendezvous Beach,** closest to the port where the ferries land. You'll find the oldest hotel on the island here, run by an interesting man named Jerry Gumbs who built the hotel 25 years ago — by hand. The hotel itself is unpretentious and has a magnetism that lures guests back over and over again. Everything — drinks, meals, suntan lotion — is kept on a tab...you keep track of it. There is a self-service bar.

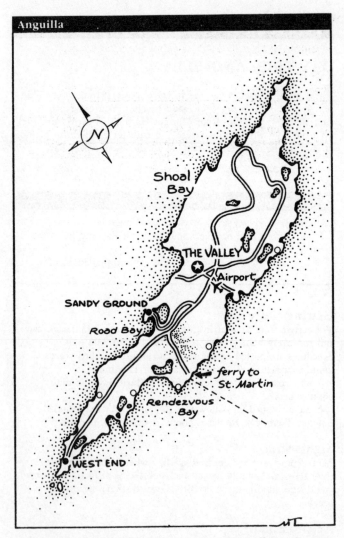

Jerry says that big hoteliers have been making offers to buy out his beach front property, still in its natural state, and replace his piece of paradise with huge resorts. He says that Christ will come again before they get their answer. 'What do they think?' he adds, 'they can just buy a place without knowing the hard work and struggle a man goes through?' Mr Gumbs does not put a price on his dream.

Elsewhere on the island, you'll find expensive hotels such as **Malliouhana,** costing £180–£360 ($300–$600) in the winter. It is said that £7.2 million ($12 million) was spent on this project.

Food

Riviera Restaurant, at Sandy Ground, Road Bay, open for lunch and dinner, is a popular terrace cafe and bar.

One of the strangest constructions is **The Barrel Stay,** a classy little joint up the beach, built entirely out of slats from rum barrels. 'The termites won't get them, that's for sure', says owner Bob Mazza. He and his partner, Jean Celis from Belgium, serve lunch and dinner; breakfast on request.

TOURS 19 – 21

SABA, 'THE UNSPOILED QUEEN'

You board the plane in St Martin. Only 15 minutes into the air, someone next to you asks, 'Is this your first time?' You nod. 'Hasn't been a wreck yet', they assure you as you tighten your seat belt. At about that time, you hear the captain announce that you're on the landing approach, and...Oh My God! They're making the wrong turn. The mountain is dead ahead of you. You think, 'We are going to crash', as you swallow hard and wish you hadn't had that bloody mary. Then a left turn and — bump — the plane lands safely once again.

You have arrived on Saba, 'the Unspoiled Queen'. Now you'll begin to see why they call the island that, as your taxi driver takes you up hills and around corners flanked by oleanders. You'll see little stone walls covered with bougainvillea, and white wooden cottages with green shutters and red tin roofs. You won't believe how clean this island is! Not a speck of paper on the ground or a bottle found anywhere. St Martin, in all its glory, is nothing like this.

If you were lucky enough to bring your other half, Saba is the place to revive romance. Except for chirping birds, a goat, donkey or two, the scene is perfectly quiet. You can hold hands and walk about the town, stopping to sample the housewives' homemade spiced liqueur, Saba Spice, heavily laden with 151 Rum. The housewives will tell you that they are not the drinking kind, but I have always noticed smiles on their faces, as if they have been checking the recipe for flavour.

They will also want you to take a look at their Saba lace, the art of drawn-thread work, which has been practised by Saban women for years. Drawn-thread work was originally introduced by Mary Gertrude Hassel, native, born on the Windwardside in 1854 and sent to a convent school in Caracas. Spanish nuns at the school taught her how to do drawn lace work. She shared this knowledge with the Saban women, who were often bored since their men were out at sea much of the time. The lacework was once among Saba's leading exports, but now it is mainly sold to tourists who stop in the little cottages and gift shops. It makes a wonderful and useful souvenir. Tea cosies, napkins, table cloths, hankies...and, if you want something custom made, the women can do just about anything. Do take a bottle or two of Spice home to share with your friends.

Suggested schedule

Tour 19   Fly from St Martin to Saba.
Taxi to your guesthouse or hotel; check in.
Take an island tour.
Make dinner reservations.
Stroll about Windwardside and The Bottom.
Stop in marked cottages to sample Saba Spice
and look at Saba lace.
Happy hour at Captain's Quarters.
Dinner

Tour 20   Breakfast at Scouts Place.
Climb Mt Scenery or go for a walk with Anna
Keene.
Take the plunge with Sea Saba or Saba Deep.

Tour 21   Shop for last-minute gifts.
Rest by the CQ pool one more day for the trip
home.
Arrange for a taxi to take you to the airport to
return to St Croix for the flight home.

Getting there

Windward Air provides the only air service, 3 times a day from
St Martin (about 9:00 a.m., 4:00 and 7:00 p.m.). Arrive at least
45 minutes early to check in. On days when the plane is over-
sold, people have been known to wait for several hours. Don't get
stuck in the Immigration line — be pushy. The homeward-bound
tourists in line may complain, but since Saba is also part of the
Netherlands Antilles there's no need to go through immigration
and you don't want to miss your flight. The flight to Saba takes
about 15 minutes and is a thrilling experience for first-time
visitors. £24 ($40) round trip.

A new method of transport is the MV *Style,* a speedboat from
St Martin that carries 50 passengers and makes the trip in 1
hour, three days a week, £24 ($40) the round trip. Tickets can be
purchased at Chesterfields, by Bobby's Marina in Phillipsburg, St
Martin, or through your hotel. Some time-shares offer free trips
on the *Style* if you visit their apartments and do the tour.

Getting around

At the airport, you'll have no problems finding a taxi. The
drivers, all very friendly, can be observed playing a mean game of
dominoes by the bar. The drivers also give day tours of the

island, £15 ($25) for a private tour or £3.50 ($6) per person with a full car. Make sure you tell them if you just want a ride to your hotel — it's a different price from the tour.

Car hire: Mr Douglas Johnson at The Square Nickel has a few new cars to hire. Also try Scouts Place (ask for Harold), the Tourism Board (Glen Holmes) or Emile's in The Bottom. The petrol station, located at Ft Bay, is only open from 8:00 a.m. to 12 noon. All have plenty of petrol to last your entire stay.

Hitchhiking is also a popular way to get from the Windward-side to The Bottom. When heading for The Bottom, just sit on the rock wall in front of the island Craft Shop and anyone going that way will stop and give you a lift. Or just start walking and put out your thumb. In The Bottom, the 'pick up' is in front of the Anglican Church.

Accommodation
Windwardside

Captain's Quarters — This former sea captain's home affords a beautiful view from its lush hillside location 500 feet above the sea. Winter rates are single £42 ($70), double £50 ($85), half board £15 ($25) extra; summer: single £33 ($55), double £42 ($70). The only hotel pool on the island is here, as well as a popular bar where devilish concoctions are made such as 'Bottoms Up', 'CQ Special' (deadly!) and the old standby, pina colada. Rudolph and Ann are the regular bartenders. Tell them Sam and Cyndy said hello! By the way, they love new joke material. There are 10-plus guest rooms at this hotel, all tastefully furnished, some with elegant 4-poster beds. Dining is al fresco, under the garden terrace pavilion. Meals include soups, salad, vegetables, main dish, tea or coffee, and dessert. Reservations are required for dinner.

Diving packages can be arranged. Contact the manager, Steve Hassel, for reservations. Tel. (011-599-4)-2201 (on Saba, just dial the last four digits).

Juliana's Apartments are located right behind Captain's Quarters. Juliana is the sister of Captain's Quarters' Steve Hassel. She offers recently built, modern apartments and rooms, nicely furnished, with private bath and use of the laundry. The Captain's Quarters pool is available for Juliana's guests. Winter rates are single £27 ($45), double £39 ($65), apartment for 4, £50 ($85); summer: single £21 ($35) double £30 ($50), apartment for 4, £39 ($65). Call Mrs. Juliana Johnson, tel. (011-599-4)-2269.

Scouts Place has 4½ rooms, usually full in season but 10 more rooms are being built. Contact Diane Medero, tel. (011-599-4)-2205. Their motto, 'Cheap and cheerful', says it all.

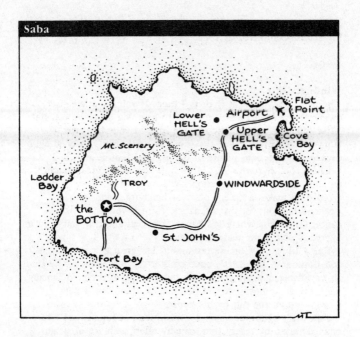

The Bottom

Cranston's Antique Inn, one of the most charming guest houses on the islands, is a two-storey Victorian house with colourfully decorated rooms, antique four-poster beds, silk-screen curtains and coverlets from the Saban Artisans Foundation. The atmosphere of this inn is not pretentious. Mr J.C. Cranston (affectionately known as 'Boose') is a happy-go-lucky sort of man who treats his guests as friends. Cranston and his son Edward ('Little Boose') have recently put a lot of work into upgrading the facilities and have built two new dining gazebos with a tropical garden atmosphere. A newly-hired Chinese chef is the rave of the island. No reservations are required. Rooms cost for a single £24 ($40), double £33 ($55). Tel. (011-599-4)-3213/3218.

The **Saba Tourism Board** puts out a list of homes and cottages for rent on a weekly or monthly basis. Contact Glen Holmes, Windwardside, Saba; or call (011-599-4)-2231. Prices tend to be much cheaper than hotels, but these places fill up fast.

▲**Royal Saban Botanical Gardens and Campground.** Camp amidst a rain forest and botanical garden overlooking The Bottom, with screened-in gazebo and bamboo shades for privacy, designer sheets on your queen-size bed, private deck, barbecue grill, sunshower off your back porch. Camping and elegance combined. Walking trails, orchid forests, tropical fruits at your fingertips. Completed in 1988.

Food

Windwardside
The best breakfast is at **Scouts Place.** If you are a late riser, owner Diane Medero may pretend to give you a ticking off, but all in fun. She can put the twinkle back in your face with fantastic omelettes cooked the way you want them, poached eggs cooked to perfection, plenty of bacon, toast, coffee and fig bananas. Tell her we said, 'Morning!' She serves great lunches, too, and dinners by reservation.

Guido's makes a decent pizza or hamburger and is the weekend hangout for disco fanatics. Even if you don't like to dance, Guido's is where it's happening. Call ahead if you're in a hurry, as pizzas are made to order.

The Chiney, a Chinese restaurant, has great egg rolls, local and Cantonese dishes. It's open daily except on Monday. Booze is also available. Things get a little rowdy there at night. A fancier, more private atmosphere can be found at the owner's new location up on the hill by his house.

Captain's Quarters makes a nice lunch of tunafish or lobster salad. Dinner, by reservation, usually offers a choice of steak, lobster, cornish hen or fish fillet. Meals come with fresh vegetables, homemade soup, dessert and tea or coffee. The candle-lit, romantic atmosphere is simple, but with a touch of class. Reservations required by 5:00 p.m.

The Bottom
Cranston's Inn has local and Chinese food, with its excellent new chef on board. Light sandwiches are offered at lunch, along with a variety of other tasty dishes. The bar is always open.

Queenie's Serving Spoon offers local food, almost always freshly prepared, so it takes a while for her to peel and cook the fabulous french fries. Call ahead for best results and prompt service. If you don't, you may wait for quite a while. Her specialities range from chicken, curried or with a hot peanut butter sauce, to fresh fish fried whole, to goat stew, always accompanied by mounds of chips, rice, pigeon peas and coleslaw.

The **Lime Time Bar** can usually fix you a light lunch. If you call by 9:30 or 10:00 a.m. and tell them what you'd like to have for dinner, Mercedes, the cook, will go shopping and make you a lovely West Indian treat.

Earl's Snack Bar sells croquettes, hot dogs, grilled cheese and beer. The **Honey Crust Bakery** has freshly baked bread (usually white), and sometimes slices of bread pudding. Pâtés are sold at **ProMart Utilities, Queenies** and **Edward's Dive Shop Bar** in Fort Bay. **Sorton's** is an interesting place to stop for a beer.

Sightseeing highlights

▲**Mount Scenery** is the Saban instant weight-loss programme. After climbing 1,064 steps to reach the top, you'll feel like you've had a serious workout. The usual time it takes tourists to reach the top is 1 hour and 20 minutes, while Sabans have set a 28-minute record. On the way, you'll pass through lush rain forest, and have a chance to stop by Johnnie Simmon's Rendezvous for a cold beer.

▲**Ladder Bay** is another strenuous walk. The route used to be the only way to get food, furniture, donkeys and cars off the boats. Located near The Bottom, just beyond Nicholson's Grocery.

▲Take a **guided botanical tour** with Anna Keene, Saba's resident horticulturist. She will take you on one of several walks, talking about plants and vegetation along the way. Walk possibilities include Mt Scenery, Sandy Cruise, Crispeen and others. It's inexpensive and well worth the price. Contact her through the Tourist Board.

▲Visit the **Royal Saban Botanical Gardens,** a newly-completed dream place. You'll pass through rain forests, beautifully-designed stone walls, colourful flowers and abundant fruits. Stop and sample mango, soursop, tamarind or Mamey's apple.

▲A **walk around Windwardside** or **The Bottom** is a sightseeing event in itself. Meet the people, stop in their houses (where marked), look at Saba lace and taste Saba Spice. Visit the Island Craft Shop, across from the Big Rock Supermarket in Windwardside, for souvenirs worth buying.

▲**The Saba Museum** on the Windwardside is a 150-year-old home filled with Victorian furniture, artifacts, books, old photographs and mementos of the island. The museum is dedicated to the memory of Harry Luke Johnson (1914–1972), whose idea it was to establish the museum. Sherry Peterson will tell you stories and explain the different artifacts you'll see. A 60p ($1) donation is suggested.

▲**The Saban Artisan Foundation,** located in The Bottom, where local women are trained in the art of silkscreening. Custom T-shirts, beautiful material, culottes, shorts, skirts and dresses are all for sale. You'll also find jewellery, dolls, Saba Spice and lace work, films and postcards.

▲**The Saba Bank** is recognised by divers around the world as one of the most exciting underwater adventures. The Underwater

Marine Park was recently completed. There are two diving shops on the island, both with certified instructors.

▲**Sea Saba**—Joan and Lou Bourque have a complete first-class diving shop on the way to St John, just outside of Windwardside, and run fascinating underwater excursions. They offer complete PADI instruction, as well as courses in underwater photography. You can see some of Joan's photos in the craft shops as postcards and 8×10 mounted photographs. Package rates are available through Captain's Quarters, tel. (011-599-4)-2246.

▲**Saba Deep** is run by Edward Arnold, formerly of Rhode Island, USA, with ancestors from Saba. Headquarters for this diving experience are at Fort Bay, where Edward also sells beer, pâtés and T-shirts. His place draws a fun crowd after the dives. He offers full diving instruction, as well as multiple dives at a discount rate. Call him direct, tel. (011-599-4)-3347; book trips locally through Captain's Quarters.

▲**Boat tours** aboard the *Frolic*, with Captain Robby Hassell, can be arranged through Captain's Quarters. Fishing charters off the Saba Bank cost £150 ($250) (half day) or £210 ($350) (full day); they include lunch, drinks, bait and tackle. Four persons maximum. A one-hour round-the-island cruise costs £12 ($20) per person.

Helpful hints

Normally in the Caribbean an automatic 10-15% service charge is added to your restaurant or hotel bill; further tipping is not required. In Saba, though, this is not the practice, so please tip people according to the quality of service they provide.

The post office is located next to the Tourism Board, on the Windwardside, and in the Government Building, The Bottom. Be sure to send everything airmail. The mail may take up to 6-8 weeks.

Pick up a copy of *Saba, The First Guidebook*, by Natalie and Paul Pfanstiehl, available at the Island Craft Shop, at one of the hotels/guesthouses, or by mail order through Natalie Pfanstiehl, Saba Guidebook, 11 Annandale Road, Newport, Rhode Island 02840, USA. This invaluable guidebook contains a complete description of Saba, her people and places. Maps and illustrations included. A copy costs £4.80 ($8); add £1.20 ($2) when ordering.

OPTIONAL SIDE TRIPS

ST EUSTATIUS AND ST KITTS

If you have extra time, consider one or both of these options before returning home. (These also fit into the middle of Itinerary 2, since flights are available to Antigua via St Kitts on LIAT.)

St Eustatius

Commonly called 'Statia' (pronounced 'STAY-sha'), St Eustatius is a flat, scrubby island with a charm that remains hidden to me, but others love it. Try it for a day and experience it for yourself. I found the main virtue to be the friendly people.

'Statia' is known in history as the first island to acknowledge the new fledgling country of the United States with a cannon salute. Stop by the tourist board in town for a copy of the historical tour, which takes about an hour and a half. We found a grave in one of the cemeteries with a real skull and crossbones embedded in the marker, evidence of the island's early pirate days.

Getting there: Windward Air flies a round-trip from St Martin and Saba to Statia, daily (scheduled times vary). Pick up a Windward timetable at the airport.

Accommodation: If you decide on an overnight visit, we recommend **The Golden Era,** a new hotel next to The Old Gin House, much cheaper and comfortable enough. Mr Lyfrock is trying to pick up business and will be most accommodating. Local food served here, well worth a try.

Most visitors are drawn to the elegant charm of **The Old Gin House.** We wouldn't recommend it as a casual visit during the high season. It's usually packed with guests who regard themselves as the 'in people'. . . and thinks its *mah*-ve-lous! The bar has a quaint, pub-like atmosphere. You must make a reservation for dinner, no exceptions, but drinking can be quite spontaneous and you may meet an interesting, well-travelled crowd.

For those on a budget, try **Richardson's Guest House.** There are 3 rooms, one with its own bath, £12 ($20) per person includes use of the kitchen. Mr Richardson also runs a taxi service.

Food: If you sleep past 9:30 a.m., you've probably missed breakfast, so try **Super Burgers,** in town, for an egg and cheese sandwich. Good burgers too. Stop in during your walk and chat with owner Kenneth Mitchell. Open 8:00 a.m.-11:00 p.m., 7 days.

Also, you could look into **Florida Ice Cream,** next to the synagogue path, or **Kool Corner** for some ting or beer.

The Golden Era offers local food. Be sure to make a reservation at **The Old Gin House** early in the day if you plan to eat there. Meals are expensive but widely raved about.

Attractions: Fort Orange and the historical buildings along the Walking Tour. Concerning the beaches, Zeelandia is rough and not very well cared for (lots of litter). The best beach is by **The Old Gin House;** a good diving shop can also be found there.

St Kitts

St Kitts used to be called St Christopher (a la Columbus), but the name was shortened in 1623 when the British claimed the island. Over the years, the island has changed hands several times. It was finally ceded to the British in the Treaty of Versailles. Brimstone Hill is testimony to the many battles fought over the island. St Kitts achieved independence in 1983.

The island's main income has traditionally been from agriculture. Sugar cane trains can be seen carrying the crop across the island, and there are a few working plantations in the countryside. Many of the old plantations have been renovated into quaint hotels, some a bit stuffy but charming just the same. Frigate Bay is the main tourist beach, and until recently the best beaches were inaccessible and distant. The island government, in an attempt to draw more foreign investors and tourism, is in the process of building a new road to the Southeast Peninsula, where calmer seas and pretty beaches lie.

Getting there: Fly Windward Air from either St Martin or Saba. Both flights go through Statia first. LIAT also has several flights to St Kitts from various islands.

Accommodation: Fairview Inn is one of the original hotels. It is an 18th-century great house, with a beach nearby, a very good restaurant featuring local cuisine, 2 bars, golf, tennis and watersports. Winter, single £36–£42 ($60–$70), double £42–£48 ($70–$80); summer, single £24–£30 ($40–$50), double £36–£42 ($60–$70). Tel. 809-465-2472/3.

Ocean Terrace Inn was recommended by our friend Joan Salmon, taxi driver in Antigua and a native of St Kitts. A small chalet hotel, OTI has all the amenities of a resort with the personal touches of a local inn. There are 2 pools, a jacuzzi, 2 restaurants and 2 bars. Tel. 809-465-2754.

Fisherman's Wharf serves the best West Indies buffet on the island, every Friday. Entertainment several nights a week. It is located in Basse Terre, a mile from the main shopping area and two miles from the airport. Tel. 809-465-2754. Summer, single £23–£45 ($38–$75), double £30–£57 ($50–$95); winter, single

£30–£66 ($50–$110), double £36–£85 ($60–$150).

Food: Paradise Pizza & Deli—On Frigate Bay, next to Island Paradise Beach Village. Friend Joan Salmon brags about the wonderful pizza, probably because **Paradise Pizza & Deli** just happens to be owned by her brother Vernon Viera, a St. Kittian lawyer. Joan's sister owns a bakery, **Patisserie,** in town.

Victor's Hideaway gets great reviews and serves local food at reasonable prices. At 9 Stanton Street, Basse Terre.

You may also eat at the **Fairview Inn** or the **Ocean Terrace Inn.**

ITINERARY 2

TOURS 1 – 7 Follow Itinerary 1, starting with **St Martin,** and going on to **St Barth, Anguilla** and **Saba.**

TOURS 8 – 10 Spend your first day on **Antigua** visiting historic English Harbour and Nelson's Dockyard. Wander through the old restorations—the Admiral's House Museum, the Admiral's Inn and Copper and Lumber Store. Visit the National Park's library, Clarence House and Shirley Heights. Walk along the harbour and have a look at the yachts. The next day, lie in the sun at Dickenson's Bay or Hawksbill (4 beaches, one of them nude), or both. On Dickenson Bay, try The Buccaneer for dinner and jazz sessions. On Tour 10 visit St. John's for shopping.

TOURS 11 – 13 Catch the morning flight to **Montserrat.** Explore town. Hop on a bus and drive up the coast, swim at Carr's Bay, catch the bus back in an hour or two, have dinner at the Iguana. On Tour 12, explore The Great Alps Waterfall, Galway Soufriere (active volcano) and Galway Plantation. Do some walking. The next day visit Air Studios.

TOURS 14 – 15 Fly out early to **Dominica.** Hire a car and have a leisurely lunch at Papailotte, 20 minutes from Roseau and by the Trafalgar Falls. Wander about the lovely gardens, sit in a warm mineral pool. In the afternoon, walk around town, visit Tropicraft, the Women's Coop, the tourism bureau for books, a map, pamphlets and information. Dinner at La Robe Creole, or your hotel. On Tour 15, drive to the Emerald Pool, then to the Carib Indian Reservation. Wander around and talk to the Indians, look at their straw work, these are the last Carib Indians around.

TOURS 16 – 17 Take the 7:35 flight from Canefield Airport to **St Lucia** or spend another day on Dominica. Either way, relax by the pool or at the beach, do some diving or anything you want.

TOURS 18 – 21 Fly to **Barbados,** take a taxi to Worthing Beach. Check into a guesthouse (unless you choose the 'naturist' way). Spend a day at the beach. Harrison Cave is first on the Tour 19 agenda. Walk around Welchman's Hall Gulch, see the Flower Forest and/or Andromeda Gardens. For Tour 20, breakfast at the waterfront, shop while it's not so crowded and head for the beach in the afternoon. Visit Barbados Windsurfing Resort, *the* centre for windsurfing in Barbados.

TOURS 1-7

ST MARTIN – ST BARTH – ANGUILLA – SABA

Check with your travel agent for the best flight deals to St Martin. You may be able to arrange a return flight direct from Barbados avoiding the need to make the long trip back to St Martin. Apex returns to St Martin range from about £500 in the winter to £585 in the summer. Book well in advance.

St Martin – St Barth – Anguilla – Saba

Turn to Tours 14 – 16 in Itinerary 1 and follow the rest of that itinerary, visiting St Barth, Anguilla and Saba. Then, instead of returning home, fly on to Antigua and continue to Tour 8 on the next page.

St Martin to Antigua

After flying back from Saba to St Martin, take one of the several LIAT flights to Antigua. (If you bought LIAT's 'Super Caribbean Explorer' it will cover all your island-hopping transport from Tour 7 on and bring you back to St Martin.)

TOURS 8-10

ANTIGUA

Antigua, a 108 square-mile coral island full of nautical history,
produced untold tons of sugar cane throughout the 18th and early
19th centuries, largely by means of slave labour. In the mid
1800s, there were 35,000 slaves and 2,500 European colonists.
According to John McPherson's book *Caribbean Lands,* sugar so
dominated land use that residents imported all other foods and
supplies. A major sugar can depression in the 19th century hurt
Antigua badly. Remains of windmills and bushes now cover
hillsides where profitable crops once grew.

To the south of the island lies English Harbour, the base for
the Royal Navy during the late 1700s and 1800s. It is also known
as Nelson's Dockyard (after Admiral Horatio Nelson). You'll find
many of the original buildings of Admiral Nelson's day now
converted into quaint hotels and pubs like the Admiral's Inn and
Copper and Lumber Store. There are many yachts, big and small,
to envy. You'll wonder if there isn't a pirate or two lurking
about, sipping a brew in one of the taverns. But alas, no pirates
remain, just your average run of the mill boat rowdies. You'll
laugh if you have the chance to help an inebriated sailor back to
his dinghy. The song 'What Do You Do With a Drunken Sailor?'
might have been written about Nelson's Dockyard on a Saturday
night.

Suggested schedule	
Tour 8	Fly in from St Martin
	Visit English Harbour / Nelson's Dockyard:
	The Admiral's House Museum, the Admiral's
	Inn and the Cooper and Lumber Store, the
	Clarence House and Shirley Heights.
Tour 9	Bask in the sun at Dickenson's Bay or
	Hawksbill Beach.
Tour 10	Taxi over to St John's, the capital of
	Antigua, for shopping and sightseeing;
	Or take a side trip to Barbuda.

Getting there
Fly from St Martin on LIAT or BWIA.

Getting around
Taxis—Look up our friend Joan Salmon, a driver at the airport. A really tremendous lady, she will give you as good a deal as possible. With a few people, it's cheaper. She'll also teach you how to play Warri, a popular game among the drivers and a great souvenir to take home. The fare from the airport to Nelson's Dockyard is £7.50–£9.00 ($13–$16) one way.

Car hire—The taxi drivers' association has several cars for hire at the rate of about £24 ($40) a day. You'll need to purchase a temporary Antiguan licence for £6 ($10), and you are responsible for the first £360 ($600) damage unless you purchase additional insurance. You'll find the stand near the airport.

Buses—A reliable bus system runs between St John's and Nelson's Dockyard Monday to Friday. Cost is about 30p (EC $1.35). Pick up and drop is outside the gates of Nelson's Dockyard, and anywhere along the way, to the Westside Station in St John's across from the market.

Sightseeing highlights
▲**Nelsons Dockyard and Shirley Heights**—This is the most fascinating place to spend your time in Antigua. The history is reflected in the restoration of the 200-year-old buildings. Women sell their wares by the entrance. Flour sack shirts and drawstrings are one of the best deals. You can get fried chicken and johnny cakes cooked on the spot. See how it's done from the lady who sits on the wall. Spend at least a day here. Visit the National Park's library, admire the collection of old books and brush up on your history of the area. Lecture tours are given on the early history of Antigua every Thursday at 4:00 p.m. For information, call the Department of Tourism.

▲**St John**—Shop and eat your way through the town. Half a day, twice, or one whole day is worthwhile here. Sights of interest include the Saturday market (arrive early), the Courthouse, St John's Cathedral and cemetery, the archives on Newgate Street, the Botanical Gardens where you can play cricket, the deepwater harbour and the rum distillery.

Activities
▲**Beaches**—There are supposedly 365 beaches on Antigua, one for every day of the year. My favourites are Dickenson's Bay and Hawksbill Beach Resort. The latter has 4 beaches, one of them nude. (If you are there in January flies can drive you nuts.) From Nelson's Dockyard, you can take a ferry to the nearby Inn at English Harbour or to Falmouth Harbour.

▲**Diving shops**—The most recommended are located at St James Club, run by Bert, and Dive Antigua at Hawksbill and Halcyon

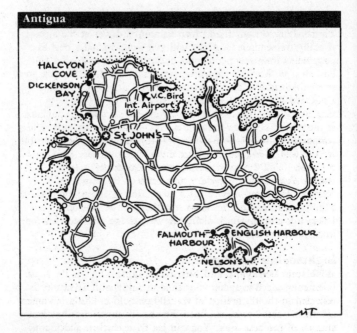

Cove Hotels.

▲**Snorkelling**—Take the Yacht Tour offered by Antigua by the Sea, up the coast from Jolly Beach Hotel, along 16 miles of coastline. You'll see underwater gardens, and old forts, visit a private island and eat well. The cost is £30 ($50). Call Basil Hill, tel. 462-4882.

▲**Day trip to Barbuda**—Several boat charters are available for fishing and diving. Island tours are offered for £55 ($90), including picnic, beach barbecue and airfare. Tel. 461-3641 after 6.00 p.m., speak to Keith.

▲**Jolly Roger Party Boat**—Drinks, calypso dancing, swimming, snorkelling, partying. Check at your hotel or call 462-2064.

Accommodation

The historic **Copper and Lumber Store,** a quaint, very British small hotel in a restored Nelson's Dockyard building, plays chamber music softly throughout the courtyard and public areas. All fourteen suites, with kitchenettes, have been refurbished with authentic Georgian period furnishings. The pub serves typical English lunches and dinners, Scotch eggs, pâté plates, cheeses and fruit platters, and has a good wine selection. Gordon Gutteridge delights guests with his dry wit. Rooms cost £50–£95 ($85–$160) a night in winter and £36–£66 ($60–$110) a night in summer. Boat service is provided to the nearby beach. Tel. 31058 or write to PO Box 184, Nelson's Dockyard, Antigua.

The **Admiral's Inn,** built in 1758 and also in the Dockyard, originally warehoused pitch, turpentine and lead. It is now restored as a comfortable hotel with one of the most popular bars in the Dockyard. Rooms cost, winter: single £33–£40 ($55–$66), double £41–£47 ($68–$78); summer: single £25–£29 ($42–$48), double $29–£34 ($48–$56). Ethelyn Phillips is the manager, tel. 809-463-1027. She also manages the **Falmouth Harbour Beach Apartments** not far up the road, where 25 self-catering apartments are available for (winter) single £41 ($68), double £48 ($80); (summer) £29–£36 ($48–$60).

For a local feel, try **The Corner Hotel and Restaurant.** The rooms are clean and air-conditioned. Amenities include a TV lounge, video system, dining room and bar serving local native dishes and the biggest roti in town. Be sure to tell them if you don't want bones in the chicken roti.

Buccaneer Cove offers 6 seaside cottages with 4 beds each, kitchenettes, bath, fans, The winter rate is £72 ($120), summer £42 ($70), for 4 persons. The barbecue restaurant features jazz and steel bands, crab races, and a happy hour from 4:30 to 6:30 p.m. There's mini supermarket on the premises. On Dickenson Bay, tel. 462-0959/2173.

Hawksbill Beach Hotel, with four beaches, cosy rooms with half board, and free watersports, feels more like a resort. For £720 ($1,200) a day, the beautiful Caribbean-style Great House on its private bluff accommodates up to 6 people in 3 bedrooms, living room and kitchen. Our thanks to the Hawksbill Hotel who pampered us midway, during our busy research schedule.

In St John's are the **Stephandale Hotel** and the **Joe Mikes Hotel.** Both have doubles for £23 ($39). No frills but clean hotels.

Food and nightlife

You'll find small, very sweet Antigua black pineapples everywhere. Try them!

Local food and drinks are served at the **Dubhie** (pronounced 'doobie'), an unusual joint with a name that sounds like one, in the landlocked boat outside the Dockyard entrance.

Pizza in Paradise has a good seafood pizza, but expensive at about £7.50 (EC $36). It is located about half a mile from the Dockyard entrance.

The Galley Bar, by the yachts in Nelson's Dockyard, is a favourite haunt for big and small yacht crews. Fun happy hour, barbecue chicken, hamburgers, chips.

The Inn, up above the Dockyard area, has a fantastic chef who comes up with some very tasty recipes. Try the orange tomato soup. Specialities such as a leg of lamb and mint pastry, beef Wellington, lobster thermador and fresh fish are also served.

Shirley Heights Lookout is the place to be on Sundays when they have a steel band, lots of good food and a barbecue. It's also a good spot to be when the sun goes down. There's a fully stocked bar; fresh fish and lobster are served. The prices are reasonable. Russell, the owner, enjoys a good chat.

Buccaneer Cove, on Dickenson Bay, is run by the sister of Shirley Heights' owner. This is my favourite place for grilled lobster, chicken and ribs. Excellent prices, informal atmosphere, and it's right on the beach. A jazz band plays several nights a week and on Sundays.

The Plantation Inn has good food and a well stocked bar. Be sure to take enough change with you, they never seem to have enough on hand. It's right across from **Dubarry's,** at the Barrymore Hotel, which several people have recommended to us—give it a try.

TOURS 11-13

MONTSERRAT

You'll feel welcome the moment you arrive at Blackburne. Montserrat has such friendly people that after two days you'll find yourself fitting into the local scene, and when your visit ends you'll have to drag yourself away. Montserrat has escaped the typical tourism scene. 600 medical students live on the island — and do they love to have parties!

The drive from the airport will take you past lush hills and mountainous backdrops. Papayas, mangoes, bananas and coconut palms grow prolifically. Montserrat was originally settled in 1632 — by the Irish. Names such as Joe Morgan Hill, Galway Plantation, Kinsale and St Patrick show the strong Irish influence — 'a little bit o' heaven dropped in the sea', as they say. Your passport is stamped with a shamrock bearing the words 'The Emerald Isle'.

Suggested schedule

Tour 11
Fly to Montserrat.
Taxi to town, check into hotel.
Arrange car hire for Tours 12 and 13.
Explore town.
Hop on a bus up the coast, swim at Carr's Bay, catch the bus back in an hour or two.
Dinner at the Iguana.
Pub crawl.

Tour 12
Explore the island in your rent-a-car, do some walking:
Great Alps Waterfall.
Galway Soufriere (active volcano).
Galway Plantation.
Dinner at Chez Nous.

Tour 13
Visit Air Studios, tour by appointment only (tel. 5678).
At times there are connections to Dominica from Montserrat; check current schedule, or else make the trip through Antigua or Guadeloupe. (Take afternoon flight to Antigua. Check into hotel closer to the airport, early flight following day.)
Have dinner and get some rest. Arrange taxi to pick you up in the morning.

The island is not a touristy place, and the West Indian culture still thrives. There are a few simple resorts, small hotels and guesthouses in town. An assortment of apartments and private homes are also available for rent in Montserrat. Most can be found in the area called Old Town. Old Town has many beautiful homes, attractively landscaped gardens and swimming pools. Contact one of the agents listed in the **Accommodation** section below for information. Stay in town to be within walking distance of restaurants and pubs at night.

Montserrat is the home of Air Studio, one of the most sophisticated recording studios in the world and an elite hideaway for performing musicians. Groups such as Duran Duran, Sting, Police, Air Supply, Paul McCartney and Elton John have recorded here. Some of the stars stay secluded and spend all of their time at the hillside retreat, while others can be found mingling in town, creating a party wherever they go. Contact Yvonne Kelly, the studio manager, for a tour appointment, tel. 491-5678.

Getting there
Airlines flying from Antigua to Montserrat include BWIA, LIAT and Montserrat Air.

Getting around
Taxis are available at the airport, in the town centre, in front of the Government buildings, and at most hotels. If you choose to see the island by taxi rather than hire car, pick one driver and agree on costs of possible excursions in advance. The information given by the taxi driver is worth the price if you're not looking for a make-your-own-pace day. Taxi fare for island scenic tours is about £4.50 (EC $20)/hour.

Car hire — Pauline Jeffers hires cars on Amersham Road in Plymouth, tel. 809-491-2345; or check with the Montserrat Tourist Board, tel. 809-491-2230; you can also inquire at your hotel. A Montserrat driver's licence can be obtained at the airport or the police station. Drive on the left.

Buses — Buses run from the roundabout by the big ice cream parlour front in Plymouth, or hail them along the way. About 60p (US $1) will take you to St John's or Carr's Bay.

Accommodation
We suggest staying in town if you want nightlife. It's a pleasant walk, anywhere.

The Wade Inn on Parliament Street in Plymouth has clean, comfortable rooms, twin beds and a bath. Winter rates are single £21 ($35), double £28 ($47) with breakfast £23–£34 ($39–$57);

half board £28–£46 ($47–$76). The 7% government tax and 10% service charge are included. Local native dishes, served Monday to Saturday, include mountain chicken (huge frog legs, found only in Dominica and Montserrat). There are also crab races and a Friday buffet with a steel band.

The Flora Fountain Hotel is a modern place catering to businessmen. A bar and restaurant are on the premises. Winter rates are single £30 ($50), double £45 ($75), half board £12 ($20) extra; summer, £24–£36 ($40–$60). Tel. 809-491-3444/3445.

The Lime Courts Apartments, located in a plantation-style house, has 8 guest apartments (one or two bedrooms), fully furnished, with kitchen, patio and private bath. Tel. 809-491-3656.

For apartments or private home rental, call **Jaquie Ryan,** PO Box 425, Plymouth, Montserrat, tel. 809-491-2055, or **Neville Bradshaw,** PO Box 275, Plymouth, Montserrat, tel. 809-491-5270.

Sightseeing highlights

▲**Great Alps Waterfall** — From Plymouth, it's a ten-minute drive to the start of a 30-minute walk to the 70-foot-high falls. A guide is recommended; guide fees are £3.50 (EC $15) single, £2.50 (EC $10) per person for couples. Taxi charge £6.50 (EC $30) for waiting and return fare.

▲**Galway Soufriere** — A short, exciting hike to the steaming, sulphurous centre of the volcano. The taxi waiting and return fare is £10 (EC $45).

▲**Old Fort on St. George's Hill** — Breathtaking views of the surrounding areas from the plateau. Taxi round trip fare £4 (EC $17).

▲**Bird Sanctuary** — Nesting colony of birds such as egrets, herons, coots, gallinules, cuckoos and kingfishers. Taxi round trip fare £3 (EC $12).

▲**Galway Estate Ruins** — Tour an old sugar boiling house, sugar mill and related buildings. Taxi waiting and return fare £8.50 (EC $40).

▲**Chance's Peak Climb** — For the more energetic and adventurous, a 3,002-foot climb to the top of the island's highest peak. Contact the Tourism Department for special arrangements.

▲**Bransby Point Fortification** — See restored cannons and enjoy scenic views of the surrounding areas. Taxi round trip fare £3.50 (EC $14).

▲**Government House** — Tour the grounds, Monday, Tuesday, Thursday and Friday, 10:30 a.m.–12:00 noon. Tour the house on Wednesdays only, 10:30 a.m.–12:00 noon.

▲**Montserrat Museum** — Historic relics housed in an old sugar

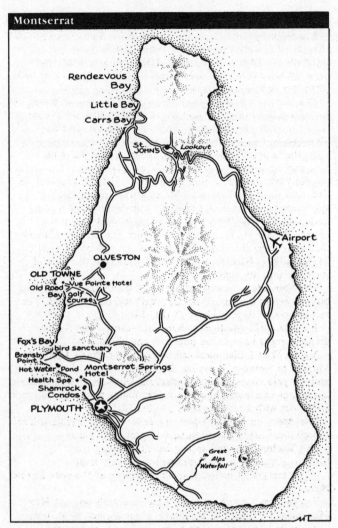

mill. Sundays and Wednesdays, 2:30 p.m. – 5:00 p.m. For special groups, call 5443.

Food and nightlife
The Iguana is among our favourites for a casual atmosphere and gourmet fare such as deep-fried camembert served with mango jam about £1.70 (EC $8), pizza and great chicken liver pâté.

There's also a quiet garden setting at the back. Always an interesting crowd here.

Across the street try **The Plantation,** another popular bar for the medical students. Hours are flexible so if you don't find it open, go somewhere else and come back later — the owner caters more to a late-night fun crowd.

The Oasis, next door to the Plantation Club, is best known for its 'mountain chicken' — huge frog legs that resemble chicken but have a more delicate flavour. The owner is an expatriate Canadian.

Another enjoyable mealtime treat is the **Wong Gee Cat** (formerly named, and still referred to as, Chez Nous), located in 'Upper Parliament' upstairs behind Ram's Market. You have to look hard for it the first time. We ended up in someone's apartment (well, the door was open); they were very understanding The Wong Gee is owned by an Englishman, Glenn. He and his West Indian cook turn out fantastic Chinese food with a few alterations. Their huge egg roll (about £1 (EC $4) looks like a burrito. A good crowd gathers at the bar and stays late into the night.

The **Nepcoden,** located in Weekes, is primarily a night club, but also serves the best (if not the only) roti on the island. The taxi trip to get there is about £1 (EC $4).

Students at the **Medical School** informed us that Sunday dinner there is open to the public — and cheap.

A good West Indian meal can be had at the **Wade Inn,** Monday to Saturday. A typical dinner might be chicken, curried mutton, pork chops, mountain chicken, red snapper with bananas, salt fish or goat water stew. On Friday nights there is a crab race and buffet with a steel band for £5 (EC $22).

The Attic, on Marine Drive, serves local food, breakfast, lunch and dinner. Guests are encouraged to play their piano.

The Yacht Club in Wapping has great snapper and hamburgers, and features a different dish every night.

If you can get an invite, visit the **Montserrat Defence Force Bar.**

You can get a tasty goat water stew, weekends only, at **Mrs Morgan's** little shack in St. John's. No frills, just great stew.

If you find yourself at Carr's Bay, be sure to stop at the **Psychedelic Bar.** You can get Ting, Vienna sausages and crackers. A popular haunt for the medical students, the name speaks for itself.

TOURS 14 – 16

DOMINICA

This is the largest, most rugged and mountainous of the
Windward Islands. You won't find fancy resorts here. Instead,
Dominica has rain forests, tropical ferns, waterfalls and 365
rivers. This corner of paradise especially pleases outdoors-people.
Opportunities abound for walking, mountain climbing,
photography, scuba diving and birdwatching.

In the middle of the Hurricane Chain, Dominica has taken
more than its share of beatings from Mother Nature. In 1979,
only six months after gaining independence from Great Britain,
the island was devastated by Hurricane David. Roads were
washed out, houses collapsed and forty people died. Even today,
many locals date events 'before' and 'after the hurricane'.
Rebuilding has been slow; roads and buildings are still being

Suggested schedule

Tour 14	Fly out early to Dominica. Arrange for car hire. Enjoy a leisurely lunch at Papailotte, by Trafalgar Falls, 20 minutes from Roseau. Wander about the lovely gardens, relax in a warm mineral pool. Pamper yourself for waking up so early. Walk around town — visit Tropicraft, the Women's Co-op, the tourism bureau for books, a map, pamphlets and information. Dinner at La Robe Creole or at your hotel.
Tour 15	Drive to the Emerald Pool. Stop at the Emerald Guest House for a lemonade, beer or light lunch. Drive on to the Carib Indian Reservation, wander and talk to the Indians, look at their straw work. These are the last Carib Indians anywhere. Drive from the reservation up the coast, around the north side of the island to Plymouth. Visit the Cabrits.
Tours 16 – 17	Take a side trip to St Lucia or spend more time on Dominica.

restored with US, Canadian and French aid. Agriculture provides almost all revenue and employment, and plantations are only now beginning to recuperate. Dominica remains among the most economically disadvantaged nations in the Caribbean — and the most beautiful.

Note: Dominica (pronounced 'Do-mi-NEE-ka') is not related to the Dominican Republic. Only the names are similar.

Getting there

Fly into Dominica at Canefield Airport near Roseau, not the larger Melville Airport on the opposite side of the island, to save the long £10 ($18) taxi ride to town. You can fly there on LIAT from Montserrat via either Antigua or Guadeloupe. If you want to work Guadeloupe into this itinerary (see the end of this section), now's the time to do it.

Transport

Hire a car at **Valley Rent-A-Car** in Roseau, tel. 809-448-3233, or your travel agent can arrange it through Whitchurch Travel Agency in Roseau, Telex 8650 WHTRVL.

Dominica Tours offers photo safari tours, birdwatching, boating tours, water sports, car rentals, transfers, sailing, scuba diving, hiking, mountain climbing and flower tours. Talk to Janice Armour at 809-448-2638/9.

Safari tours can also be arranged through the Emerald Pool Hotel (see **Accommodation**). Your cab driver can arrange tours by the hour. Road maps can be obtained from the Dominica Tourism Bureau in Roseau.

Accommodation

Our favourite hotel in Roseau is **Reigate Hall,** on a hilltop overlooking the town. £30–£45 ($50–$75) (winter) includes full English breakfast. There's 24-hour room service — the night guard, a good cook, caters to your late-night emergency food needs. For a super bit of extravagance, one room has its own party hot tub, bar, TV, stereo and VCR. Owner Gordon Harris, who spent £1¾ million ($3 million) renovating this former guest house, can tell you what to see and do in Dominica. You'll usually find him around the bar at cocktail time. Harris, an eccentric young Englishman, still drives a Rolls-Royce Silver Shadow despite the road leading up to his hotel. Tel. 448-4031 or 4033.

Other hotel possibilities in Roseau:

The **Evergreen Hotel** has ten comfortable, simple rooms with showers, phones and air conditioning, some with private balconies. Homelike atmosphere, family-style dinners, laundry

services, scuba equipment and air refills. £30 ($50) half board
(single), £42 ($70) (double). Tel. 809-449-83288. Mona Winston,
Mgr.

The **Anchorage Hotel,** on the coast half a mile from Roseau
and 2 miles from Canefield Airport, has 26 clean, simple rooms,
2 double beds each, showers and air conditioning. Restaurant
(great Sunday lunch), swimming pool, squash court; on the water
— no beach. Year-round rates are £24–£30 ($40–$50). Owner
Janice Armour also runs Dominica Tours. Tel. 809-448-2638.

About ten miles from Roseau, **The Castaways** has huge
rooms, 2 double beds each, simple furnishing, showers and air
conditioning. Good local food. Like all Dominica hotels, this one
needs a new coat of paint, but the beauty outside more than
compensates for the lack of interior decor. Winter rates are single
£42 ($70), double £55 ($90); summer: single £36 ($60), double
£50 ($80); all rates are half board. American-born manager Linda
Harris is loads of fun and, while helping you plan your stay, can
show you the off beat side of Dominica. Tel. 449-6244.

For out-of-town accommodation, you can't beat **Papailotte
Hotel** at Trafalgar Falls. Anne Jean Baptiste and her husband
Cuthbert have worked hard to create an atmosphere of tranquil
beauty. There are just four guest rooms, comfortable and cabin-
like with lovely Dominican quilts. The food is fantastic, the
surroundings even better. Single rooms are £21 ($35) with no
meals, £33 ($55) half board; double rooms are £30 ($50) with no
meals, £55 ($90) half board. Tel. 809-448-2287.

Springfield Plantation is a great getaway spot — a beautiful
mountain setting in the middle of nowhere — what a view! Large
rooms with antique furniture, great location for walking and river
bathing. Year-round rates are single £39 ($65), double £57 ($95)
half board; apartments may be rented for £180–£240
($300–$400) a month. Three miles from Canefield Airport, Tel.
809-449-1401/1224.

Delightful **Emerald Pool Guest House** lets you choose
between the guesthouse and an A-frame in the woods. No
electricity; candles and lanterns are provided. Year-round rates
are single £8 ($14), double £10 ($18) with no meals (half board
£17–£26 ($28–$43)). One week full board including a 3-day
safari costs single £230 ($386), double £300 ($496). Call manager
Gina Staehli at 809-448-8095.

Layou Valley Inn has clean, simple, modern rooms and (we're
told) 'bloody good' food. Rates are no meals £15 ($25) single, £24
($40) double; half board £27 ($45) single, £48 ($80) double; full
board £32 ($53) single, £58 ($96) double.

Food

Dominican food specialities include 'bakes' (johnny cakes), 'bouldchaw' (curried fish salad), fried 'sprats' (smelt), 'titi-ri-acre' (deep-fried fishcake), 'farine' (avocado and red beans), 'smokey joes' (smoked herring), 'boudin' (black pudding or blood sausage), soused bananas, and parsleyed dasheen. You can sample all these at once at the **Anchorge Hotel's** Sunday lunch.

If price is no object, **La Robe Creole** is the best restaurant in town: Creole food, gourmet West Indian dishes, homemade ice cream. The **Reigate's** chef, who formerly cooked for the King of

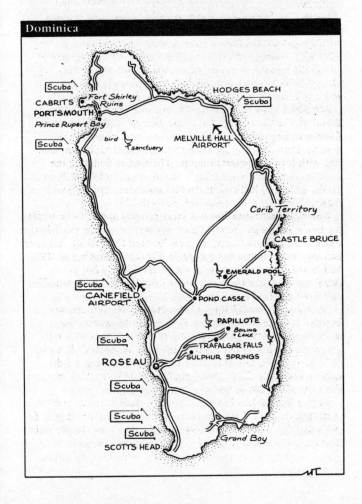

Dominica

Scuba
CABRITS — Fort Shirley Ruins
PORTSMOUTH
Prince Rupert Bay
HODGES BEACH
Scuba
Scuba
bird sanctuary
MELVILLE HALL AIRPORT
Carib Territory
CASTLE BRUCE
EMERALD POOL
Scuba
CANEFIELD AIRPORT
POND CASSE
PAPILLOTE
BOILING LAKE
Scuba
TRAFALGAR FALLS
ROSEAU
SULPHUR SPRINGS
Scuba
Scuba
Scuba
SCOTTS HEAD
Grand Bay

Belgium, does excellent steaks, Crab Farci and giant local crayfish. For quality snacks, try **The Mouse Hole,** on the side of La Robe Creole and run from the same kitchen, or **The Orchard,** a local favourite where you can get rotis, chicken, mountain chicken (frog legs) and crab, with soft jazz in the background.

Reasonably-priced local food can be found at **The Easy Restaurant, The Green Parrot** or **Guiyave.** Your best bet for eating out, though, is one of the guesthouses — try **Evergreen Guesthouse** or **Kent Antoine Guest House** — where you can eat family-style; reservations are required.

Ask the locals if there's anything exciting going on at night (most of the time there isn't).

Lunch at the **Papailotte Restaurant,** surrounded by a surrealistic tropical rain forest where sculptured gazelles and swans hide among ferns and fromeliads, is delightful. Try the breadfruit puffs and the flying fish creole, with a rum punch. (See the falls first — you may feel too relaxed to walk up there after lunch.)

Sightseeing highlights

▲**Roseau** — Check out the 44-acre **Botanical Gardens**; photograph the smashed school bus, permanently merged with a tree during the great hurricane. Shoppers, take a look at the hand-woven straw rugs in **Tropicafts Women's Co-Op** on Turkey Lane.

▲**The Emerald Pool** is the centerpiece of **Morne Trois Pitons National Park,** about 3½ miles from Pond Casse on the road that leads to the town of Castle Bruce. Have your hotel pack you a picnic lunch or stop by The Mouse Hole. Plan to swim. This is a romantic spot — but avoid it when the tourist ships are in.

▲**Trafalgar Falls** are worth a visit, and the Eden-like gardens of nearby Papailotte Hotel are even better. Stop there for lunch; if your're on your best behaviour Anne Jean Baptiste may show you her private trail, lush with orchids and tropical flowers.

▲**Carib Indian Reservation,** north of Castle Bruce on the island's east coast, is the home of the only remaining Caribs in the Caribbean. Stop and meet them. You'll find good buys on baskets and other local handicrafts.

▲**The Cabrits (Fort Shirley Ruins)** near Portsmouth is a renovated old fort.

▲**Boiling Lake** is interesting if you like hot sweaty hiking. Start at Laudat, a half-hour drive from Roseau. The hike (4-hour round-trip) takes you up the hills, into the mountains, through the aptly-named Valley of Desolation, to one of the world's largest boiling lakes.

Activities

▲**For the birds** — Dominica has 135 species of birds, including the endangered Sisserou (Imperial) Parrot and Rednecked Parrot which are found only on this island. The Indians traditionally hunted parrots for food and export, but since Hurricane David destroyed much of the island's forest, Protection Laws have been enacted to save the remaining bird population. Nesting time is between February and June. Animal life includes wild boars, frogs, opossums, crabs, manicous (a marsupial with a kangaroo-like pouch) and agoutis (a large rodent). Watch out for birds and wildlife in the Emerald Pool, Trafalgar Falls and Boiling Lake areas. You can learn more about Dominica's bird and animal life by stopping for a chat and a copy of the booklet *Wildlife of Dominica* at the Forestry Division, Ministry of Agriculture, located by the Botanical Gardens in Roseau. Serious birdwatchers will want James Bond's book *Birds of the West Indies*.

▲**Canoe trips** up the Indian River are available near Portsmouth for £6 ($10) per person. For information, ask Joan Armour at the Anchorage.

▲**Scuba trips** can be arranged through Dominica Tours. The best locations are noted on the map. Reportedly many 17th and 18th century shipwrecks lie offshore, including some yet to be discovered.

Optional side trip: Guadeloupe

If you have extra time, you can stop over in Guadeloupe on your way from Montserrat to Dominica.

Guadeloupe caters to resort tourism and, if you speak French, you can really experience the smaller fishing villages, the out-of-the-way places, and the people. If you don't speak French, you may find that language frustrations limit your enjoyment of Guadeloupe. The city is big and touristy, so you may be most comfortable lying on the beach or listening to jazz at night in one of the intimate cafes — both activities equally available on other islands. Guadeloupe offers good shopping for food and clothing. Stock up on inexpensive French wine, baked goods, cheeses and other foodstuffs that are hard to find on other islands.

If you do speak conversational French, your choices are much greater. The Tourism Association has lists of families who offer homestays for a modest fee.

Guadeloupe has a reasonable bus system throughout the island. Buses run from the airport every half hour; the bus stop is in front of the K Dis Supermarket, or wave one down. Mopeds are a popular method of transport, as are bicycles — if you know where you're going. Hitchhiking works if you can clearly pronounce your destination. Taxis are expensive.

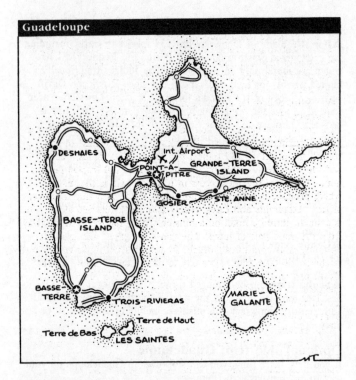

About 13 miles East of Pointe-a-Pitre is the town of Sainte Anne, with one of Guadeloupe's prettiest beaches. The Club Med Caravelle located here has a French/English language lab for those who want a brush-up course. Bicycle hire is available by the entrance of Club Med.

Towards Saint Francois, you can stay at **Hotel Mini Beach,** tel. 88-21-13, or at one of the bungalows on the edge of town, 88-20-92. Camping is permissible near the **Hotel Mini Beach.**

If you plan to visit **Les Saintes,** the outer islands off Guadeloupe, you may want to spend time at La Grande Anse, near Deshaies, first. This is where the **Club Med Fort Royal** is located. La Grande Anse has coconut palms and everything you'd expect on a great beach. Camping is available at **Camping des Sables d'Or,** La Grande Anse. Sites are very well kept, with showers, toilets, kitchen and barbecue grill.

Club Med beaches are available for day use for a fee. Club Meds are a more expensive option for one or two nights' stay, but meals and watersports are included, and the crowd is generally fun. The main virtue of these resorts is that you don't have to deal with the language problem — but you won't really get to experience the island's uniqueness there.

Ferry boats travel from Trois-Rivieres and Les Saintes between the hours of 8:30 a.m. and 4:00 p.m. Passage takes one hour and costs about £3.50 (46 francs). Air Guadeloupe makes the flight twice daily, 7:30 a.m. and 4:00 p.m., for approximately £21 – £24 ($35 – $40). Schedules are subject to change.

Terre-de-Haut is the main town, a fishing village with lots of local colour and few cars. You can hire a bicycle or moped for a day of touring on your own. Bicycles are for hire next to the church for under £3 (30 francs) per day, £5 (50 francs) deposit and mopeds are available by the docks for £3 (30 francs) per hour. There are several grocers in town as well as the market where produce is sold in the mornings. You'll also find a variety of tiny restaurants and cafés. **Hotel Bois Joli** (tel. 596-995-2553) is a small, intimite hotel on a hillside with a natural setting, away from the main part of town. The views are great, and it's only a 5-minute walk to a nudist beach. Room rates with half board start at about £50 (496 francs) per day for 2 persons. **Jeanne d'Arc Hotel** is a small 10-room hotel on the beach. It's plain and inexpensive. Seaside dining and watersports are available. It's in the village, one mile from the airport. The manager is M. Boutanquoi, tel. (596)-99-50-41.

The beach, Plage de Pompierre, is about 1 mile from Terre-de-Haut. Take a road up over the hill behind the church — a great walk. The beach is on a sheltered inlet. Admission is 10p (1 franc), and you can buy barbecue fish, fruit and juices on the beach.

Optional side trip: St Lucia

St Lucia is characterised by two volcanic peaks (The Pitons) that bear a striking resemblence to Dolly Parton. The country combines pretty coves and beaches, with a lush dramatic interior, and banana plantations among the hills and ravines produced by the island's volcanic origin.

In the vicinity of the yacht marinas (Marigot Bay and Rodney Bay) are restaurants, bars and resort life. You'll find much of what's special about St Lucia by hopping on a bus and riding through the villages when workers are on their way home, and by walking around Castries for a day having a look at the food stores and market place, and meeting people.

Castries has few older historic buildings because the city was destroyed by fire several times.

Getting there: Small planes fly into Vigie Airport, near Castries on the northwest shore of the island. The larger Hewanorra International Airport is on the southern tip of the

island in Vieux Fort. The taxi ride through the interior from
Vieux Fort to Castries or Rodney Bay takes 1 to 1½ hours and
costs about £21 ($35). LIAT flies into both airports. To avoid the
taxi fare (though the scenic beauty is worth the price), make sure
you can fly into and out of Vigie.

Accommodation: The **Islander Apartments** (tel.
809-452-8757) are comfortable studios with air conditioning,
kitchenettes and living/dining room areas, only a short walk to
fun bars and restaurants, across the street from the St Lucian for
beach and water sports.

The **St Lucian** is a former Holiday Inn (and the rooms still
look like it) with all-inclusive watersports — snorkelling, skiing,
parasailing, etc. It's a fun place, but expensive at £90 ($150) per
night in the winter season. You can get your hair and nails done
here if you're in need of a perk-up. The food is less than
exciting. The bars aren't too bad at all and sometimes offer jazz.

Anse Chastanet, tucked into a hillside overlooking the beach,
is great if you want isolation. The 37-bed accommodation
includes 10 suites (6 with plunge pools), a beach, good
snorkelling, windsurfing and tennis, all with a great view of the
Pitons. Winter rates are single £67 ($112), double £80 ($132);
summer: single £43 ($72), double £53 ($88); half board £17 ($28)
per person extra. Tel. 809-454-7355.

In Vieux Fort stay at **The Cloud Nest,** a charming guesthouse
that feels like grandma's bedroom — all chintz and crocheted
doilies from years and years of collecting. The meals are
outstanding and so is the conversation. Ask them to make you a
platter of the local produce. The rooms are inexpensive.

Food: The **Islander** in Rodney Bay has good lobster. Art deco
Capone's serves Italian cuisine on one side and pizza on the
other — moderate to expensive. **Pat's Pub** and **The A-Frame,**
both in Rodney Bay, are happy hour favourites of the yacht
crowd.

Rain on Columbus Square in Castries is quaint, Victorian and
casual. The porch upstairs has good breezes. Rum drinks are
great. The food — sandwiches and full meals — is local style with
a special flair. **The Green Parrot** is *the* fancy place to dine:
entertainment, floor show, great food.

Doolittle's in Marigot Bay offers open-air dining. It's a good
local island spot and yachting hangout. The film *Dr Doolittle* was
made around here in 1966. Gorgeous surroundings.

Activities: The colourful market is in one of the few remaining
historic buildings in Castries. You'll want to take a picture, but
don't unless you've got permission from your subject. The ladies
generally dislike having their photos snapped. Tipping is
appropriate.

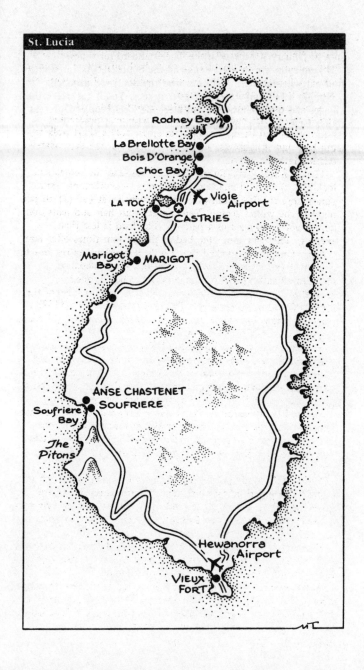

Cricket season is February to June, and soccer season runs from July to January. Check with the Tourist Board for times.

Hiking spots are in the Pitons and the Soufriere. Ask around to find out whether the hot springs near the Soufriere are open.

Hop on a bus and travel wherever it goes. You'll get to see the villages and neighbourhoods and meet the local people. Different routes have different bus stops, all in the same vicinity. When in doubt, ask for help — the friendly St. Lucians are more than willing to give directions.

TOURS 18-21

BARBADOS

Our Bajan taxi driver put Barbadian history in a nutshell: 'The Spanish ran the Indians out, the English ran the Spanish out, then the Barbadians ran the English out'. Independent since 30 November 1966, Barbadians have a real knack for putting things together. Most of the hotels are on the west coast, including some quite exclusive ones that ooze with luxury. The architecture and construction materials are similar to Bermuda or the Bahamas. Service is a plus on this island, and the locals are well trained in gracious hospitality. The Barbadians have a flair for attracting the tourist pound — and give you a good product in return.

Barbados depends on tourism — yet, thanks to good planning, has confined most tourist-related industry to the west side of the island, with some on the south, leaving the rugged, hilly east coast for Barbadians. The average tourist, lying in the sun and sipping rum punches, will never see this territory, so make the most of your inside information and venture out to see the whole country.

It is undoubtedly better to visit Barbados during the off-season, to avoid the masses and find more reasonable prices. Yet at any time of the year you can stay at an eminently affordable guesthouse and enjoy your vacation at least as much as those who pay exorbitant prices.

Suggested schedule

Tour 18	Taxi to Worthing Beach and check into your guesthouse. Spend the day at the beach.
Tour 19	Hire a care or a taxi and visit: Harrison Cave. Welchman's Hall Gulch. The Flower Forest and Andromeda Gardens.
Tour 20	Breakfast on the waterfront, then shopping. In the afternoon, head for the beach or the Barbados Windsurfing Center.
Tour 21	Last-minute souvenir shopping. Final beach day.

The lush interior of the island is covered with field after field of sugarcane. If you drive through the fields before the 8-foot-tall cane has been harvested, you'll feel as if you were about to be swallowed and lost, but the roads are easy to follow. Further toward the east side of the island you'll find very rugged country and the rough Atlantic Coast offers great surfing.

Getting there
Both LIAT and BWIA fly to Barbados from Dominica as well as St Lucia and most other nearby islands.

Sightseeing highlights
Shopping and food here are trip highlights in themselves. Excellent duty-free buys can be found in Bridgetown.

The Tourist Bureau can provide you with a tourist attractions and activities list as long as your arm. Here are my favourites:
▲**Harrison Cave** is an interesting natural phenomenon, as long as you get there when no cruise ship tourists are around. A small cart takes you through the caves as a guide points out interestingly lit stalactites, stalagmites and underground pools.
▲**Welchman's Hall Gulch** offers pleasant walking trails where you can observe the local flora and fauna.
▲**Andromeda Gardens,** a private garden and greenhouse, is far less touristy than Flower Forest. Ask for a tour. Located not far from Tent Bay on the eastern coast. Mick Jagger ordered thousands of plants from here for his house on Mustique.
▲**Flower Forest,** maintained as a tourist attraction, is serene and beautifully manicured. The gift shop offers a variety of unique souvenirs, cookbooks and clothing.

Accommodation
There are several little guesthouses in Barbados: no frills, but clean and generally more personable than the big hotels. Guesthouse operators know that you're not too fussy, so you get special treatment...which fussy people don't get.

Summer Place by the Sea is located on Worthing Beach. There are 7 rooms, some with king and queen-size beds and down pillows. A family atmosphere prevails. Owner George Mattos says that you can walk all the way out to the reef without getting into deep water. The white sand beach, ½ mile long, is as pretty as you'll find. All this costs only £6 ($10) single, £11 ($18) double in the summer; winter rates are £9–£15 ($15–$25). Breakfast costs £2 ($3.50), and dinner £4.50 ($8). The chef, a local Barbadian who has been in George's employ for 15 years, serves an excellent selection of local food. There is an outdoor sink for laundry, as well as a clothesline. In the high season,

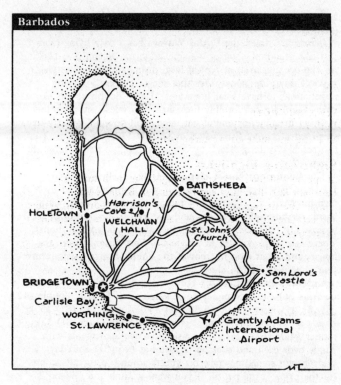

telephone ahead to ensure that you'll have a room. If you don't, you might want to investigate the two guesthouses next to Summer Place by the Sea. With Lawrence Gap to the east and Rockley Beach to the west, you can be sure to enjoy your stay nearby, particularly at the various swimming pools. Tel. 809-428-6983/6620.

Next door to Summer Place is the **Diamondville Guest House,** run by Brenda Parkinson. You'll enter through the beach side where she has attempted to keep a little front yard with lots of plants and a simple walkway. There are 5 rooms: 3 doubles with own bath, 2 rooms with single beds and access to facilities. Rates are £10 (BD $35) per person for doubles and £8.50 (BD $30) for singles, meals included. Bed costs only £4.25 (BD $15), with bed and breakfast for £6 (BD $20); there is a 5% tax. Breakfast is at 8:00 a.m. Between 12:00 and 1:00 p.m. you'll get a 'nice plate of soup', and between 5:00 and 5:30 p.m. you'll be served a 'heavy' dinner. The whole schedule changes on Sunday. You'll be offered a copious lunch at around 1:00 p.m., along with tea and cakes between 6:00 and 7:00 p.m. The Carib Beach, a good local dive, is nearby.

Across the street, the **Rydal Waters** has a cosy living-room just like grandma's house. We smelled curry pigeon peas cooking for the evening meal of typical local dishes served homestyle. Joyce Talma, the owner, says that she is 'currently making negotiations to have solar hot water'. Her 6 double rooms (2 twins each) are comfortably furnished, and guests may use the washing machine, or one of her maids will do your laundry for a small extra charge. Prices start at £6 (BD $20) per person. You can reach Worthing Beach by cutting through a path, across the street.

The **Beaumont Guest House,** tel. 427-0139, located in Hastings, is a big, airy older home, well kept and owned by Mrs. Cynthia Marshall. There are 4 rooms with 2 beds each, wash basin, reading light, 2 chairs, and a shared bathroom for every 2 rooms. £10 (BD $35) per person includes breakfast and dinner. There is a path to Palm Beach, just a short distance from the house, and a bus stop in front of the house. Many guests return year after year, so call ahead.

Gideon's Inn & Lobster House, tel. 428-5363 has 8-rooms, no frills but clean. Summer rates: single £6 (BD $20), double £12 (BD $40); winter, single £8.50 (BD $30), double £15 (BD $50). Meals are discounted to hotel guests: breakfast £1.75 (BD $3), dinner £4.25 (BD $15). They also offer two apartments with 2 single beds each and cooking facilities at £15 (BD $50)/day. Gideon will sometimes take his guests around to the attractions for the price of the petrol. If you want a drink and Gideon is busy with the restaurant, just offer to help yourself. Gideon's is an old Barbadian home on the ocean, next to Sandy Beach Hotel and opposite Star Discount Store.

In **The Sandy Beach Hotel** rooms have king size beds, fully equipped kitchen, living room, patio, TV and telephone. It is a very comfortable place to stay in Barbados, within walking distance to the Lawrence Gap area restaurants and bars. The flying fish served at the **Beach Side Grill** is great for breakfast. Only one of two licensed vendors are allowed to sell flying fish to visitors. This is a great place for families who want a little more comfort, but not too fancy. Hotel Reservations: 809-428-9033/1.

Barbara and Murray Chandler, tel. 809-435-4027, have 8 apartments for naturists (clothing optional), with a large pool and jacuzzi, located in the parish of St Phillip. £24 (BD $80) per couple includes kitchen facilities, twin beds and maid service. There is also a great little Chinese restaurant and bar. You can use the facilities for £12–£24 (BD $20–BD $40)/day, and camping is permitted for £12 (BD $20). It's just 5 minutes from the airport — call if you want to be picked up. If you wish to stay longer, the apartments cost £300 (BD $1,000)/month. Murray says that nearby Long Beach is a good nude beach — but keep an eye on your clothes, they have been known to disappear.

Restaurants

The Pot and Barrel, at the entrance of Sam Lord's Castle, offers fried chicken (a regular box costs £2.20 (BD $7.78), a 9-piece thrift box £4.95 (BD $17.36), great for a day's picnic lunch at Long Bay; also, great roti for £1 (BD $3.50), family-size pizza with 5 garnishes for £5.35 (BD $18.76), and a good pina colada £1.40 (BD $5).

In Bridgetown: At **The Fisherman's Wharf,** cocktails, appetisers and dinner for two can be had for £18 (BD $60). Try the 'pastelle' — like a tamale, made of cornmeal, filled with a tasty meat mixture and wrapped in banana leaf. At Christmas time, the pastelles are filled with fruits, prunes, etc. Tamborri chicken is a good choice, as is fresh grilled fish. Easy on the Bajan hot pepper sauce. I love it, but it's not for everyone.

Pisces Restaurant, a great spot, serves Caribbean seafood with a contemporary twist — e.g. blackened dolpin (not the porpoise, but the fish also called dorado or mahi-mahi) or grilled kingfish (try the curry sauce). Fresh coconut pieces are given to all patrons at the bar. There's a nice selection of wines.

Return home

If you're on a LIAT excursion, you can fly back to the originating island and catch a plane home from there.

If you don't feel like returning home quite yet, read on.

ITINERARY 3

This itinerary is the most flexible of the three, allowing time to hop between small islands on whim. As you venture down through the Grenadines, the notion of keeping to a definite schedule will seem increasingly absurd. By the time you reach Grenada, you probably won't even know for sure what day it is.

TOURS 1 – 4 Fly to **Barbados** and follow Itinerary 2, Tours 18–21.

TOURS 5 – 14 Fly from Barbados to **St Vincent.** After exploring the island, begin a week-long island-hopping cruise via mail boat from St. Vincent to Grenada, visiting **Bequia, Canouan, Mayreau, Union Island, Carriacou** and/or **Petit Martinique** along the way. Choose which islands appeal to you most. How long you stay on each depends on the day of the week when you start: boat service to all except Bequia is twice-weekly.

TOURS 15 – 18 Explore the island of **Grenada** with its spice factories, forest reserves, waterfalls and fishing villages. Despite its 1984 turmoil, you'll find Grenada completely safe, serene and idyllic.

TOURS 19 – 21 Fly to **Trinidad,** where you'll find the Caribbean's richest mix of cultures as well as calypso and steel band music galore. A quieter atmosphere can be found on Trinidad's nearby island, **Tobago.**

TOURS 1-4

BARBADOS

Check with your travel agent for the best flight deals to Barbados. You may be able to arrange a return flight direct from Trinidad avoiding the need to make the trip back to Barbados. In any event LIAT can be used to carry on your island hopping. Apex returns to Barbados booked three weeks in advance range from £400 in the winter to £550 in the summer.

For this part of your holiday, turn back to Itinerary 2, Tours 18–21, starting on p.87.

TOURS 5 – 14

ST VINCENT AND THE GRENADINES

Forget everything about keeping a schedule while you are in the Grenadines. The pace is slow on all of the islands, so allow yourself to sink into 'Caribbean time'. The Grenadines are the place to get lost — for at least a week, maybe more.

Each island in the Grenadines has its own personality. You can make a whole day out of going to the beach, finding a nice spot for lunch, and meeting the friendly local people.

Some of the islands are expensive private resorts where relaxation is given first priority. They offer privacy and a kind of barefoot elegance. You don't have to pay a fortune to have a similar experience. You'll see big yachts that charter for £5,000 ($8,500)/day, parked next to small sailboats that charter for £60 ($100)/day. The prices may vary drastically, but everyone mingles, swims at the same beach, and shares the common goal of getting away from it all.

An increasingly popular method of seeing the Grenadines by sea is to hop aboard the mail boats and ferries which are bound for Bequia daily, and down-island twice weekly. You'll share passage with young boys flogging peanuts and lemonade, muscular young men hoisting the sails and loading cargo, a Rasta drinking milk from a coconut, women with their heads wrapped in brightly-coloured scarves, assorted locals and tourists, piles of cargo, and an occasional goat or two. The experience is great!

Suggested schedule

For the remainder of this trip, the only schedule you need is the one you make for yourself. Enjoy yourself!

Mail boats: St Vincent and The Grenadines

The mail boats listed below provide inexpensive inter-island transport. Down-island from Bequia, the boats only run twice weekly, so if you always travel in the same direction you must spend three or four days on each little island where you stop. But the boat, the *Grenadines Star,* goes south one day and north the next, so the strategy for stopping on more than two islands in a week is 'two forward, one back'. For example, cruise south from Bequia to Mayreau on Monday, then north to Canouan on Tuesday, and on south to Union Island on Thursday. The only days when you can't get off the smaller islands, heading either direction are Wednesday, Saturday and Sunday.

My Edwina (motor vessel): Monday – Saturday, departs Bequia 6:30 a.m., arrives St Vincent 7:30 a.m., departs St Vincent 12:30 p.m., arrives Bequia 1:30 p.m.

Friendship Rose (island schooner): departs Bequia 6:30 a.m., arrives St Vincent 7:45 a.m., departs St Vincent 12.30 p.m., arrives Bequia 1:45 p.m.

Grenadines Star (motor vessel):

Monday & Thursday—departs St Vincent 10:00 a.m., arrives Bequia 11:00 a.m.; departs Bequia 11:15 a.m., arrives Canouan 1:15 p.m.; departs Canouan 1:30 p.m., arrives Mayreau 2:30 p.m., departs Mayreau 2:45 p.m., arrives Union Island 3:05 p.m.

Tuesday & Friday—departs Union Island 7:00 a.m., arrives Mayreau 7:20 a.m.; departs Mayreau 7:30 a.m., arrives Canouan 8:30 a.m.; departs Canouan 8:45 a.m., arrives Bequia 10:45 a.m.; departs Bequia 11:00 a.m., arrives St Vincent 12 noon.

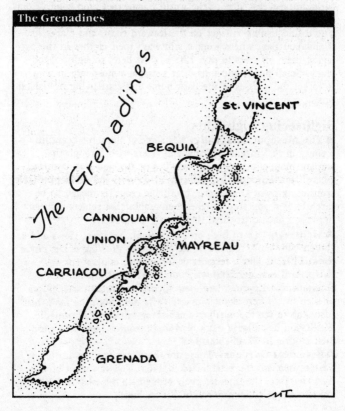

The Grenadines

Saturday—departs St Vincent 12 noon, arrives Bequia 1:00 p.m.
(No service on Wednesday or Sunday.)

Obedient (motor vessel) departs Union Island 7:45 a.m., arrives
Carriacou 1:00 p.m., Mondays and Thursdays.

Fares: Between St Vincent and Bequia, £1 (EC$5); between St
Vincent and Canouan, £2 (EC$10); between St Vincent and
Mayreau, £2.50 (EC$12); between St Vincent and Union Island,
£3 (EC$15); between Union Island and Carriacou, £2 (EC$10).

ST VINCENT

St Vincent is the largest of the Grenadines, and by far the most
mountainous and fertile. Rich farmlands provide a major source
of income. Mesopotamia Valley is where you'll find most of the
agricultural areas. 90% of the world's arrowroot crop comes from
St Vincent. Bananas and breadfruit are also valuable cash crops.
You'll find fishing villages on the leeward coast, and places like
Wallilabou Bay, where women still wash their clothes in the bay,
laying them on trees to dry. Life is good here, though not too
fancy. Small hotels and inns offer a casual atmosphere in which
to forget the stresses of life back home and start living on 'island
time'.

Sightseeing highlights
▲**The Mesopotamia Valley** has some of the most beautiful
scenery in St Vincent. Streams and rivers rush through the
verdant mountain valley, and you'll pass through rich farmland
where bananas, coconuts, dasheen, arrowroot, and other profitable
crops are grown. One of the 'profitable crops' is illegal, so be
careful when you stop to take photographs that someone doesn't
think you have discovered their marijuana patch.
▲**Montreal,** located high on a mountain, has great views and a
garden with pink, red and white anturiums growing under citrus
trees. There is also a restaurant, a pool and mineral springs.
▲Up the **Leeward Highway** you'll find small towns such as
Questells and Layou, where petroglyphs and rocks carvings can
be seen by a river, about a quarter of a mile from the main road.
Also stop to see the whaling and fishing village of Barrouallie.
Wallilabou has a large batik workshop; women there still wash
their clothes in Wallilabou Bay.
▲**Botanical Gardens**—These are the oldest gardens in the
western hemisphere, established in 1765. You can see a bread-
fruit tree from the original plant brought to the island in 1793 by
Captain Bligh of *Mutiny on the Bounty* fame.

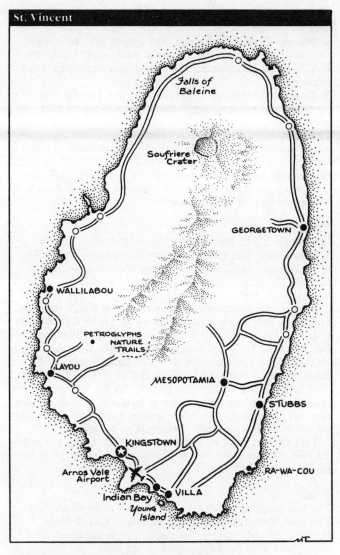

The **Archaeological Museum** in the Botanical Gardens has interesting artifacts, old stone tools and pottery.
Fort Charlotte affords a good view of the Grenadines and

Kingstown. Built in 1806, the fort is only a few minutes' drive from Kingstown.

St Vincent Craftsmen Centre, just a short walk from downtown Kingstown, has a wide variety of locally-made handicrafts, West Indian dolls and items handcrafted from straw, clay, wood or coconuts.

St George's Cathedral in Kingstown, a fine example of late Georgian period architecture, features beautiful stained-glass windows.

The Falls of Baleine, 7½ miles north of Richmond Beach, are accessible only by boat. Check with the Tourist Board or your hotel.

Buccament Valley—Nature trails at the head of the valley go through a tropical rain forest. You might get to see (or hear) a St Vincent parrot or a whistling warbler.

Transport

Mini buses depart from Market Square to all of St Vincent's outlying areas. Fares are cheap, about 20p–80p (EC$1–EC$4). Just wave them down, and they'll stop. Wallilabou, on the Leeward Coast, costs about 40p (EC$2) and so does Mesopotamia, while Layou costs about 30p (EC$1.50).

  Car hire can be arranged at your hotel or at **Kim's Rentals Ltd,** tel. 61884; **David's Auto Clinic,** tel. 71116; **Car Rentals Ltd,** tel. 61862/1614; **Star Garage,** tel. 61743; or **Johnson's U-Drive,** tel. 84864. You'll need a driver's licence from St. Vincent, which you can get at either the Police Station on Bay Street or the Licensing Authority on Halifax Street. When I was there last, this was not always enforced. The fee for non-residents is £2 (EC$10). If you do hire a car (a great idea for a day), make sure you ride around town before heading to the hills. Some cars are not in the best condition. Driving is on the **left.**

  Taxi rates are fixed by the government. The hourly rate is £6 (EC$30). Fares to most hotel destinations are between £2.30 and £3 (EC$12 and EC$15).

Food

The best places to eat West Indian food are at the hotels. Try **The Last Resort** (formerly Coconut Beach), **Grand View, Heron** and **Cobblestone.** You might want to call ahead, since some places serve family-style meals at set times.

  The **French Restaurant** offers a more expensive menu of tasty French cuisine, seafood specialities, and good wines of course. For a more moderate price, you can get a very nice French meal at **Harbour View;** lobster and steamed seafood are favourites, along with escargot.

The private island resort of Young Island has three restaurants. Luncheon buffet offers a huge array of tasty salads, local vegetable dishes, meats and fish, all attractively presented. Take a motor launch from the Young Island Pier. A few pubs along the waterfront serve grilled chicken and fish, hamburgers, pizza, etc. The **Dolphin,** situated by the Young Island dock, is one of them; its owners also own the **Chicken Roost.** Day cruises and yacht charters are available there—call 84238.

Nightlife

During the peak season, the hotels have barbecues and steel band entertainment. Check with the Tourist Board for information. If you like casinos, travel 30 miles from Kingstown to the **Emerald Isle Casino.** There's dancing, too. Young Island has entertainment on Tuesday, Wednesday, Friday and Saturday.

Accommodation

Our favourite hotel in St Vincent is the **Tropic Breeze,** located about a mile from the airport on a hillside overlooking town. Light and airy rooms have private baths, balcony/sitting rooms and pretty views. The hotel sits in a lush garden surrounded by fruit and flowering trees. There is a patio restaurant, and a piano in the bar. It's two miles from the beach, and transport is provided daily. Two-bedroom apartments with kitchen, two baths and balcony are also available. Summer rates for rooms are single £18 ($30), double £24 ($40); winter: single £24 ($40), double £30 ($50). Apartments cost £60 – £80 ($100 – $130) a day. Tel. 809-458-4641.

The **Cobblestone Inn**: Built in the early 1800s, this former sugar warehouse has been transformed into a quaint little hotel with a popular bar and West Indian-style restaurant on the main street and a terrace on the roof. Rooms are small but comfortable and air-conditioned. A pretty courtyard downstairs has several interesting shops. Rates are reasonable, single £22 (EC$95); double £30 (EC$130). In case you're coming or going by ferry, the waterfront is right in front of the hotel. Tel. 809-456-1937 or 1177.

The **Heron Hotel**: Originally built to house visiting plantation owners and managers, this Geogian structure offers simple, comfortable lodging with a friendly West Indian atmosphere and the price can't be beaten. The rooms are air-conditioned, with private bath and phone, and the rates include breakfast and dinner. Year-round, single £20 ($33), double £32 – £36 ($54 – $60). The 15 rooms are in much demand. so you might need to call ahead, tel. 809-457-1631.

BEQUIA

Life on Bequia is easygoing, and you'll soon feel at home. Sailors
who know the Grenadines also know that Bequia is the place to
go for food. After weeks of eating callaloo, pumpkin soup and
curried everything, **Mac's Pizza** is a sight for sore eyes. Not
limited to pizza, Mac's has fresh whole-grain bread, huge sweet
buns, apple and bran muffins, salads with sprouts. Eat to your
heart's content, because you won't find those choices on other
islands. Spend some time wandering about the village. You can
stop and observe the boat builders at work on a whaling boat or
yacht. Whaling is still practised on the other side of the island.
They still use the old traditional method of rowing out to sea and
harpooning the whale by hand. Once the whale is killed, men
have to dive down and sew its mouth shut quickly before it fills
up with water and sinks. It seems like a lot of work, but it
provides a meagre living to the few who still practise whaling.

A true artform in Bequia is model shipbuilding, which can be
seen at Lawson G. Sargeant's shop. He produces exact replicas of
people's yachts—down to the last rope and dinghy paddle. His
shop is to the left of the port. Ask someone for directions.

McCarthy Phillips' rowboat taxi service will take you from the
Frangipanni to Princess Margaret Beach, or you can walk over
the hill on a trail. This beach is where you'll find **The Reef** and
the best tuna sandwich (fresh tuna!) with chips I have ever had.
Service is really slow, but it's worth the wait. Order and sit on
the beach, they'll come for you when it's ready. Try the fritters
too. Some women bathe topless here; if you're discreet, no one
objects.

One of the best bookstores in the islands, especially on subjects
dealing with the islands and sailing, is found in Port Elizabeth.

At **The Whaleboner,** you can have an outfit custom made in a
day if they don't already have what you are looking for in the
shop. Hand appliquéd pillow cases and aprons tell stories of
whaling and island life; they make nice souvenirs.

Local Color Ltd. is an upstairs boutique run by two delightful
women named Joan and Elayne. Stop by just to meet them.
Noah's Ark has some interesting woodcarvings and casual
clothing.

Dive Bequia is located at Sunny Caribe, tel. 809-458-4714 or
457-4409. The owner, a friendly young American, can suggest
several dive options during your stay in Bequia.

The elders of Bequia sit under the big tree in town. This is the
spot to pick up the latest news and gossip.

Food

Mac's Pizza and Bake Shop is known throughout all the

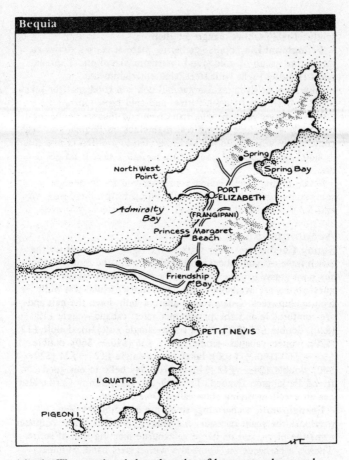

islands. We were lured there by tales of huge sweet buns and outrageous pizza. We found this and more. Mac, from Bequia, and Julie, from Canada, are warm and friendly, as if you had known them all your life. They proudly serve fresh ingredients and offer a wonderful array of baked goods daily, as well as pitas and quiche.

The **Whaleboner** is another enjoyable place for breakfast and lunch. They have homemade yogurt, good pizza, sandwiches, omelettes and fresh lime pie. The bar is the jawbone of a whale, with stools made from the vertabrae.

The **Harpoon Saloon** is a wonderful place to watch the sunset over the bay, but not so terrific when the rubbish at the dump below is being burned. Lunch and dinner are served. We recommend the lobster and chicken, as well as the lobster salad sandwiches. 'Yachties' congregate here.

Frangipanni, a popular gathering place at sunset, draws an interesting group of sailors and international visitors. Thursday night is buffet night with steel band entertainment.

The Reef at Princess Margaret Beach is a good spot for lunch. Try the fresh tuna! Conch fritters and cold beer, too.

Sunset draws yachtspeople, fishermen and tourists to the local bars and, while there are no real nightclubs on Bequia, you may come across a 'jump up' or barbecue. Go to a different restaurant or hotel each night and you're sure to find a steel band or dancing.

If you find yourself feeling poorly, or you are in need of seasickness tablets (called 'Gravol'), go up to the clinic in town and for a donation the nurse will get you whatever you need.

Accommodation

Sunny Caribe: Not a far walk to the right of the port up the beach (take off your shoes or they'll get wet), the Sunny Caribe sits on a grassy expanse right on the beach. Both cabanas and guest rooms are available in the main house, which was built from a shipwreck. Guest rooms share a bath down the hall and are comfortable and cheap. Summer rates: cabana—single £12 ($20), double £24 ($40), hotel room—single £6 ($10), double £12 ($20); winter: cabanas—single £24 – £36 ($40 – $60), double £36 – £60 ($60 – $100); hotel room—single £12 – £24 ($20 – $40), double £24 – £42 ($40 – $70). Say hello to our good friend Perkington Osgood. Tel. 809-458-4325. Sunny Caribe also has an excellent diving shop called Dive Bequia.

Frangipanni, a charming, small inn at Admiralty Bay, overlooks the yacht harbour. A former St Vincent Prime Minister owns the place, and its bar is a favourite meeting spot at sunset. There's a barbecue on Thursdays with a steel band. Summer rates are single £9 – £18 ($15 – $30), double £15 – £27 ($25 – $45); winter: single £15 – £27 ($25 – $45), double £18 – £36 ($30 – $60). Tel. 809-458-3255.

Julie's Guest House, in the heart of town, is clean and basic, and serves good island-style home cooking. Half board rates are single £9.50 – £11 (EC$40 – EC$50), double £16.50 – £21 (EC$70 – EC$90). Tel. 809-458-3304.

Transport

Taxis are available around the port or through your hotel. You can walk to most places but you may need wheels to go to the other side of the island—Spring on Bequia or Bequia Beach Club.

Water taxis: McCarthy Phillips takes you by boat to one of the beaches, or on an island tour to see Moon Hole, unusual houses built on the side of a cliff.

Day sails to Mustique are available on *Calypigion,* a 35' sloop. There may be other people willing to share a charter for the day. Check at your hotel for details.

UNION ISLAND

Union Island is a popular port of call for boating enthusiasts of all types and means. **The Anchorage Yacht Club** is the favoured watering hole and a great place to meet someone for a game of backgammon. The rum punch and daiquiris make you feel like you've been hit over the head with a hammer, so sip slowly!

Life on Union Island is so easy going... no need to hurry, it won't do any good. Some of the locals smoke a lot of ganja and tend to let life drift by.

The three small hotels on the island are all located in Clifton, the larger of the two main towns. There are a few stores and one clinic on the hill in case of illness. *Don't drink the water.* Cows are butchered right in town on the side of the road, and the meat is sold fresh—direct from the animal, enough to make a vegetarian out of anyone.

The beaches are pretty and natural. One of our favourites is the private property of Clifton Beach Hotel and Guest House's owners. Check with Marie Adams if you're interested. You may want to rent the beach house for a few days, especially if you like total privacy with no frills or nightlife. You'll have the beach all to yourself. They were planning to decorate the house when we were there last, but you'll have to get some supplies if you plan to stay. The Adams also own a grocers.

You can take a dinghy to Palm Island, or ride out with the help in the morning. This is true paradise, well worth the extravagance of £130 ($220)/night double (winter), fabulous meals and high tea included. This is barefoot elegance at its finest. Conversations with John ('Coconut Johnnie') Caldwell and his wife Mary include tales of the marijuana revolution in '79, when a few Rastas took command of Union Island for a day and attempted to include Palm Island. John single-handedly repelled the invaders with his trusty .22, as guests cheered him on and sipped pina coladas.

Accommodation

Clifton Beach Hotel and Guest House: Both the hotel and guesthouse offer clean, comfortable accommodation. The guesthouse is just a short walk away, above the grocery store, and

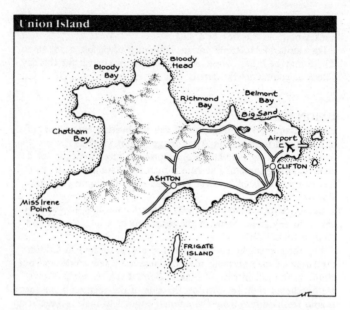

offers use of a central kitchen or meals at the hotel. There is a beach house, available for rent by the day or week. Conrad Adams and his daughter Marie offer warm hospitality and great home-cooked meals. Mr Adams' wife runs the grocers beneath the guest house. Laundry service is available. Room and guesthouse rates are half board, unless you prefer to plan meals yourself. Winter: single £19 ($32), double £36 ($60), guest house single £16 ($27), guesthouse double £30 ($50), summer: single £16 ($27), double £30 ($50), guesthouse single £14 ($23), guesthouse double £24 ($40). Tel. 809-458-8254.

Palm Island

Directly across from Union Island is private Palm Island, where you can have a real barefoot holiday with a touch of class. It's worth the trip for at least a day or two. The water is an unbelievable pale blue, and perfect for swimming. All meals and watersports are included. Meals are expertly prepared by Prince Cudoe. Have a tall rum punch with John Caldwell, a former schoolteacher and a very interesting character. He and his wife Mary turned the former Prune Island, once overgrown by manchineel trees and not very pretty at all, into a beautiful palm-covered white sand paradise and changed the name accordingly.

Rooms are large and nicely furnished. The shower is outdoors. You can see over (but no one can see in) and bathe in the sunshine. High tea, served every afternoon, is one of the nice little extra touches. Dress is very casual. Winter rates are single £90 ($150), double £130 ($220); summer: single £75 ($125), double £105 ($175). When you consider that some hotels charge £60 ($100) a night for nothing special and without meals, **Palm Island** is a real bargain. You'll be glad you stayed.

Food

Food is not a highlight on Union Island, but the best home cooking around is at the **Clifton Beach Hotel.** Meals are served family-style, and no one goes away hungry. If you want something special, just ask Marie Adams. She makes good hamburgers, chips and pizza in the snack bar, just in case you have a craving for fast food. Otherwise, go for the conch, chicken or pork chops, all served with local vegetables such as pigeon peas and callaloo or pumpkin soup.

The menu at **The Anchorage** is fabulous; unfortunately, the range of choices is limited. The sausages served at breakfast are really American hotdogs, and service is slow. The bar was their best bet on my last visit.

The food at **Palm Island** is fabulous. Take a dinghy for lunch (or dinner, but make sure you can get back).

CARRIACOU

Carriacou is a wonderfully slow, restful place. The city of Hillsborough has a small market, post office, Barclay's Bank, government and customs buildings and a few shops. The pier is the busiest place in town, but only on mail day (Saturday) and when produce comes in (Monday). During the first week of August, Regatta brings with it festivities, parties, foot races, greased pole contests, and lots of drinking. The local white rum, also known as the 'Invisible Man', is cheap, 60p ($1) for half a bottle. Among Regatta's highlights are the big drum dancers who perform on the market. The dance, passed down through African families, is now performed only on Carriacou—traditionally at weddings and other events, and as a prayer for deceased relatives.

You might enjoy watching the boat builders at work. They'll be happy to answer questions and maybe even let you lend a hand.

Sandy Island is a nice place for a picnic and an all-over tan. Have a water taxi take you out, but don't forget to make return arrangements.

Mostly, enjoy the break from the more frenzied lifestyle you left behind. It's catching!

Transport

Mail boat connections are available from Union Island on

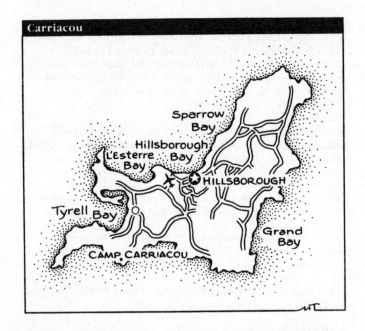

Mondays and Thursdays. Mail boats also go there from Grenada on Wednesday and Saturday, returning Monday and Thursday.

You can reach Carriacou by plane from Barbados, St Vincent, Union or Grenada on LIAT.

Food and accommodation

You might choose one of **The Mermaid's** 14 rooms with four-poster beds and a hibiscus-filled backyard. Delicious entrées include local West Indian fish and chicken dishes, and great rum punch.

The **Prospect Lodge** is owned by an American couple. Ann and Lee (both artists and creative people) very much enjoy the lifestyle this little island offers and are eager to share it with others. They will provide comfortable accommodation, good food, a library, snorkelling gear, binoculars, small locally-made boats, helpful advice and local guides. Bedrooms off the main house rent for single £9 ($15), double £12 ($20), with a 2-bedroom cottage at £33 ($55), for 3 or 4 persons or £24 ($40), for 1 or 2 guests, breakfast and dinner £9 ($15) extra. There are a 10% service charge and a 20% government tax on meals, all prices. The Prospect Lodge is located on the Leeward side of the island, two miles south of Hillsborough. For reservations, cable: Prospect,

Carriacou, West Indies; or try the overseas operator: tel.
809-443-7380. From Grenada, call 37-380.

PETIT MARTINIQUE

Like Carriacou, Petit Martinique is a parish of Grenada. For
generations, Petit Martinique has had a reputation as an island of
smugglers. However, these smuggling activities are not nearly as
nefarious as one would think. Duty-free goods—alcohol, TVs and
modern conveniences—are bought in Sint Maarten and brought to
the Grenadines; that's about the extent of it. Everyone knows that
it happens; but the attitude is that the smugglers provide a
service, so their activities are none of anybody's—especially
visitors'—business.

There are no hotels on Petit Martinique. However, the mail
boat stops here on the way between Carriacou and Grenada.

TOURS 15-18

GRENADA

Grenada is small enough to do a one-day blitz tour and see the main sights — but it's definitely nicer to take your time and capture the essence of this spice island.

You could spend your whole visit between St George and Grande Anse and find plenty to do. This is where you'll find most of Grenada's colour. Spend at least a day hanging around the harbour in St George. On Tuesdays you can watch the schooners as they are loaded with fruits, spices and crates bound for neighbouring islands. Live animals are boarded up as well, and an occasional mother-in-law.

On Saturday, market day, take your camera for a photographic field day. West Indian ladies sell local produce and Grenadian delicacies, and good buys are to be had everywhere. Stores and restaurants abound along the harbour. The National Book Store and the Grenada Teachers Supply have newspapers as well as local cookbooks (good souvenirs).

At Spice Island Perfume Ltd, you'll see a nice selection of local teas and herbs, homeopathic remedies such as the guava leaf tea, which takes the edge off a bad bout of flu.

Getting there

The MS *Eastward* is the new boat on the Carriacou run. An island-trader ship, it leaves Carriacou at 10:00 a.m., Mondays and Thursdays. (A one-day from Grenada to Carriacou and return is offered every Sunday from 7:00 a.m. to 7:00 p.m.) Captain Bedeau charges about £2.25 (EC$10) for the trip, and sells fried chicken, beer and liquor on board.

The schooners *Adelade B* and *Alexia II* also leave Carriacou for Grenada on Monday and Thursday.

Getting around

From St George, take a water taxi (small dinghy) to Grande Anse Beach, 60p (EC$3), or flag down a bus ... what a ride! Like an old college Volkswagen prank, they'll pack in as many as they can for 20p (EC$1). Taxis can be expensive, and go up an additional £2.25 (EC$10) at night.

Tours are available to show you the rest of the island. We use **Arnold's Limousine Service**. Arnold is reasonable and will help you plan your day, getting the most in for your money. He can also arrange drive-yourself car rentals.

Grenada Tours and Travel offers a unique 'People to People' programme which introduces you to a Grenadian of your

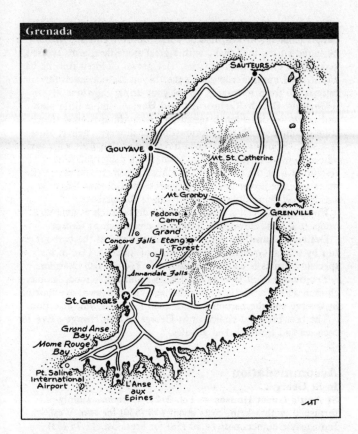

profession, adding personal insights to your visit.

Carin Otway also arranges tours, tel. 4459, and her husband is
the manager of LIAT, in case you need any flight assistance.

Take a sunset cruise on *The Loafer*, a 70-foot party catamaran,
anchored in the harbour at St George. The inexpensive price
includes limited rum punch. Stop and meet Captain Al for time
schedules.

The *Rhum Runner* is another good choice for partying at sea.
Their steel band can play the 1812 Overture!

Food

Breakfast and dinner are always good West Indian fare at **St
James Hotel**, or **St Ann's Guest House**. For a Caribbean feast,
make reservations in the afternoon at **Mama's Bar and
Restaurant**. You must have an appetite, though — mama puts

out a whole table of various local entrees, whatever she can get: lambie (conch), chicken, fish or pork, probably curried. Mama can be found sitting in a chair, with a great stone face, arms crossed, keeping an eye on the festivities. Her grown children run the bar, and it is an uproariously good time. If you are not much for bitters, tell them to leave it out of your drink; they love it!

Coconut Beach Restaurant and Bar: A simple little pink and green wooden French restaurant. Everything is good there, from a simple lunch to a glorious lobster dinner. Their chocolate mousse is fabulous. After sunbathing, try passion fruit with rum. The new owners, straight from France, are delightful. The restaurant is at the end of Grande Anse Beach. If you take a taxi, make sure the driver doesn't get you to the Coconut Disco by accident. Walking distance from Ramada Renaissance.

Nutmeg, great for a drink and local dishes such as lambie, caters to a local crowd. It's located in downtown St George.

Delicious Landing, in St George at the end of the harbour, is run by a local Grenadian with a sense of humour. One of his speciality drinks is called 'US Bomber'. Try the fish chowder.

Tropicana in St George has Chinese and creole food, lambie, chicken and fish. **Balisier** has the best view in town, overlooking St George and the harbour, and a good food and wine selection.

The best breakfast choice in St George is **The Hungry Eye** for coco tea and freshly-baked goodies.

Accommodation
In St George:
St Ann's Guest Houses — Tel. 2727. 15 rooms, simply furnished, with a bath, costs about £18 ($30) for two. West Indian-style dinners cost £4.50 ($8) for breakfast, £1.75 ($3) family style. The games room downstairs has a snack bar (hamburgers and drinks) for guests who wish to chat about their plans for the next day — a good place to find someone to share a hire car or tour. A lot of philosophical discussions occur over the pool table. If you are a late sleeper, bring ear plugs — cockerels start early. The cinema is nearby; within an easy walk to town; Grande Anse is a mile away.

St James Hotel, located in the heart of St George overlooking the harbour and a picturesque lagoon. The rooms are simple, some have private baths, others share. The restaurant serves excellent West Indian cuisine with real silver in a charming setting. In the bar you'll meet an array of guests from around the world. The shuttle bus can take you to Grande Anse. Rates are: double room only, £26 ($44) double with half board £34 ($57). Tel. 2041 or 2042.

Near Grande Anse:
Wave Crest Holiday Apartments: Nine fully furnished
housekeeping apartments, 5 minutes from the beach. In season, a
one-bedroom apartment is £24–£27 ($40–$45), two-bedroom £33
($55); offseason: £21–£30 ($35–$50). Food fair and bus stop
nearby. Mrs Joyce DaBreo, tel. 4116.

South Winds Holiday Cottages: Nineteen fully-furnished,
2-bedroom cottages and apartments, 500 yards from Grande Anse
Beach, near the food fair and restaurants. Rates are £24–£30
($40–$50) for apartments in season; £33 ($55) for cottages; off-
season, £6 ($10) less. Owner Chasley David also rents cars.
Linens are changed mid-week.

If you want more resort-style accommodation, try **The
Ramada Renaissance**, located right on Grande Anse Beach. It's
one of Ramada Inns' upgraded Renaissance hotels, and the rooms
have been beautifully furnished with deluxe amenities. Good
package deals that include the Ramada are available through
BWIA.

Beverly Flats overlooks Mourne Rouge Beach. Rates are £21
($35) per day (winter) for 1-bedroom apartment, £27 ($45) for
2-bedroom apartment; weekly rates available; summer is £105
($175). Write to Mrs Alimenta Bishop, PO Box 167, St George,
Grenada, West Indies. Tel. 2124. Mourne Rouge is a gorgeous
little beach used as a nude beach by the medical students and
locals.

Sightseeing highlights
▲**Spice Processing Plants** — Try to visit one in Grenville or
Gouyave. Ask for Augustine Straker, Quality Control and Tour
Guide, in Gouyave, or for a guide at the office. It's more
interesting than it sounds, and you'll learn a lot about nutmeg
and mace, for instance: good nutmegs sink while bad ones float;
defective nutmegs are used in Vick's ointment and creams. Mace
is a by-product of nutmeg and a natural euphoric. Supposedly,
prison inmates drink mace tea to get high. After 15 minutes of
walking around and smelling mace you'll feel fantastic.
▲**Annandale Falls** — Locals will dive from the top of the falls
for what I'd consider far too little money.
▲**Grand Etang Forest Reserve** — About 20 minutes or so
outside St George. 12 camping sites were being planned on our
last visit, down by the Grand Etang Lake. Stop in the Nature
Center for maps and information.
▲**Mount Qua Qua and Concord Falls** — Good hiking
options, North of St George's, these are a series of 3 cascades,
high in the hills. The first can be reached by road; the other two
by foot, about a 2-mile trek. Take a lunch.

▲**Fedon's Camp** — Further North, and higher up Mount Qua Qua, you'll reach the headquarters of Julien Fedon, a French-speaking mulatto who owned the Belvedere Estate during the 1795 Revolution and helped lead the rebellion against the English. He reputedly wore his boots backwards to avoid being tracked.

▲**Fishing villages** — Talk to the fishermen in Gouyave, as they pull in their day's catch. This is also the centre of nutmeg activity, with Dougaldson Plantation and the Spice Processing Plant. Not far away is Sauteurs (which means 'leapers' in French), the site where the last Carib Indians leaped to their death rather than surrender to the French. It's now a pleasant village filled with schoolchildren. In a creek a few miles from Sauteurs, a stone still bears markings made by the Caribs.

Levera has a long stretch of unspoilt beaches, worth stopping for. You can see Green Island, Sandy Island, Sugar Loaf and sometimes even Carriacou in the distance.

▲**Betty Mascoll's Plantation House** — If you have time, make reservations for lunch there. Built by her father 73 years ago, it was constructed of hand-chiselled stones, using a mortar made of lime and molasses. She serves a buffet of local-style dishes, such as pepper pot, chicken or ox tail stew. Vegetables are all from the garden. For dessert, we had guava stew with sour sop ice cream. Lunch is about £6.75 (EC $30) and there is plenty.

TOURS 19-21

TRINIDAD AND TOBAGO

Trinidad is a classic melting pot of Indian, English, African, French and Asian people, and the result is felicitous indeed. Each culture plays a different role in society, giving richness and contrast not found on other Caribbean islands.

We've found the best times in Trinidad are to be had in the panyards and calypso tents. There are many calypso tents during the period January to March for pre-carnival practice, and calypso is found in hotels year-round.

Calypso makes for an enjoyable evening in Trinidad. Nothing is sacred with calypso — especially politics and other targets of satire. The adlibbing is called 'extempto'. If you have a big nose or grey beard, someone will probably sing about it, but it's all in fun. Guys, if they sing about your 'big bamboo', take it as a compliment.

There is a whole new slang in Trinidad, called 'Ule' talk. For instance: 'Ley we go down the road an lime' means let's have a party. 'Mauvelang' is when you run someone down. Ask around and you'll pick up other catchy phrases to take home. Maybe you'll get the chance to 'jump thru the streets' (a street party).

Listen to the music at the panyards (where the steel bands practice for the forthcoming carnival) and you may be surprised at the work that goes into this kind of music. The music is carefully arranged in parts — alto, tenor, etc — and many bands have bonafide music conductors/instructors, just like a symphonic band. Trinidad's National Anthem, which opens and closes television broadcasting days, is played by a steel band.

Getting there
Trinidad-Tobago is BWIA's home base, and they offer frequent flights. LIAT also serves Trinidad.

Getting around
Port-of-Spain is a thriving metropolis, both hectic and interesting. Traffic is crazy, so I wouldn't advise a hire car here. It takes an artist to figure out the transport system. The route taxis are the cheapest; they pick people up and drop them off along a one-way route. There is a standard fare for each route, although sometimes you can get them to make a slight detour for an extra fare. There are plenty of route taxis, which you can recognize by the letter H on the licence plate of a car or maxi van.

Regular taxis cost quite a bit more, especially after 9:00 at night

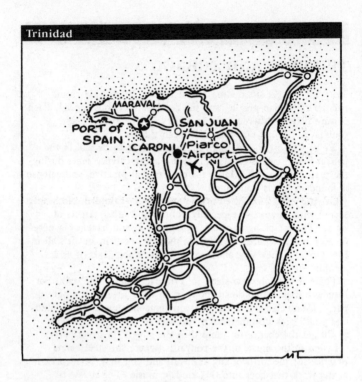

when the fares increase by 50%. Sometimes, you might not have
a choice, unless you like to walk.

Where to stay

My choice is the **Kapok Inn,** by Queens' Park Savannah.
Comfortable rooms are nicely redecorated with wicker furniture,
and some have TV. Amenities included a launderette, pool,
kitchen and two restaurants with fantastic food. It's an easy walk
from the botanical gardens and the zoo. 16 – 18 Cotton Hill, St
Clair. Tel. 662-6441 or 6444.

   The Chaconia Inn is another good choice, moderately priced.
It features three-times-weekly barbecues, pool, nightly disco, a
good restaurant and comfortable accommodations. 106 Saddle
Road, Maraval. Tel. 623-2354/2101.

   Contact the Trinidad and Tobago Tourist Board for the current
list of participants in the new bed and breakfast programme. For
a small price you can stay with locals and get a first-hand view of
life in Trinidad. You'll learn things no other tourists will – and
eat well.

Food

Tiki Village, on top of Kapok, is very classy with a Polynesian flair and the best egg rolls I've ever had. Prices are very reasonable compared to the Chinese luncheonette in town.

Mangals, 13 Queen Park East, serves spicy Indian food with Trinidadian flair in a lovely, old Victorian mansion. **Char-B-Que** offers good local side dishes, chicken and ribs.

Chavonia Inn has a barbecue three times a week about £10 (TT $45) per person.

The local hot sauce is definitely worth buying.

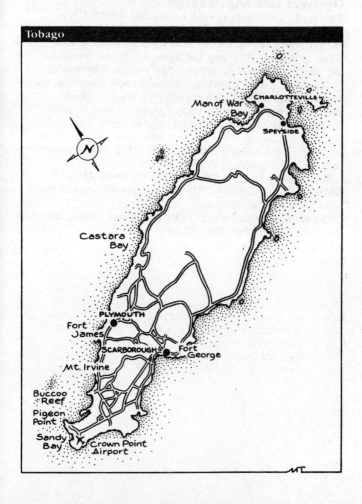

Tobago

Sightseeing highlights

Trinidad's true attractions are the people, their food, their music
and their culture. But if you have an irresistable urge to sightsee,
the **Botanical Gardens National Museum and Art Gallery**
houses Carnival costumes, old artifacts, maps and artwork. It's
located next to Mangals' Restaurant. Both Victorian mansions by
the park's edge. Walk around the centre of Port-of-Spain, and
consider a tour of **Asa Wright Nature Center** or **Caroni Bird
Sactuary.**

Optional side trip: Tobago

This lovely little island is *much* calmer than Trinidad, less
citified, ideal for relaxing. To get there, take LIAT (or include it
in your BWIA ticket). Ferries (slow ones) are also available.

Stay at **Man-O-War Bay Cottages,** run by our friends Pat
and Charles Turpin. Lovely private self-contained cottages on
Charlotteville Estate, a working 1,000-acre cocoa plantation, they
sit among lush tropical gardens right on a beautiful beach.
Everything you need for the perfect getaway is here — scuba
diving, snorkelling, deep-sea fishing, guided nature tours, birdwatching and hiking. It's a 5-minute walk to local shops. Rates
are 1-bedroom £18 ($30), 2-bedroom £36 ($60); 3-and 4-bedroom
units are also available. Tel. 809-639-4327.

Blue Waters Inn (tel. 809-639-4341) and **Della Mira
Guesthouse** (tel. 809-639-2531) are both inexpensive, and the
latter has a popular night club.

The most frequented tourist sights are **Lovers Beach, Bucco
Reef** and **Bird of Paradise Island.**

INFORMATION & INSIGHTS

Check with your travel agent regarding passport and visa requirements as these may vary. Exchange rates quoted below are of course approximate.

US VIRGIN ISLANDS

The US Virgin Islands are an archipelago with three major islands — St Croix, St Thomas and St John — and about fifty islets. Formerly a Danish colony, the islands were bought by the Unitied States in 1917 and remain an unincorporated US territory.

St Croix: Size: 84 square miles, the largest of the US Virgin Islands. Population: 55,000.

St Thomas: Size: 28 square miles, including Charlotte Amalie, the capital of the US Virgin Islands. Population: 47,000.

St John: Size: 20 square miles, two-thirds national park. Population: 2,500.

Currency: US dollars.

Language: English.

For more information contact: US Virgin Islands Tourist Office, 16 Bedford Square, London WC1B 3JA, tel. 01-637-8481.

BRITISH VIRGIN ISLANDS

A territory of 36 islands, 16 of which are inhabited, the British Virgin Islands have been a British colony since 1666. The capital is Road Town, Tortola.

British Virgin Islands: Size: 59 square miles total. Population: 11,500.

Currency: US dollars.

Language: English.

For more information contact: British Virgin Islands Tourist Board, 26 Hockerill Street, Bishops Stortford CM23 2DW, tel. 0279-54969.

ST MARTIN

The world's smallest territory shared by two sovereign nations, St Martin was colonised by both France and Holland in the early 17th century. The French side is a subprefecture of Guadeloupe, governed by France. The Dutch side, Sint Maarten, is a part of the Netherlands Antilles, a parliamentary democracy that belongs to the Kingdom of the Netherlands.

St Martin (French side) — Size: 21 square miles. Population: 15,000.

Currency: French franc. 1 franc = approx. 8p; £1 = approx. 12.5 francs.

Sint Maarten: (Dutch side) — Size: 16 square miles. Population: 15,000.

Currency: Netherlands Antilles florin (guilder). 1 florin = approx. 32p; £1 = approx 3.13 florins.

Languages: French, Dutch, English.

For more information contact: French Government Tourist Office, 178 Piccadilly, London W1V 0AL, tel. 01-493-7622.

ST BARTHELEMY

St Barthelemy ('St Barth' or 'St Barts') was settled by the French in the late 17th century. Traded to Sweden in 1784, the island was the only Swedish colony in the western hemisphere for nearly a century before France repurchased it. Today it is a dependency of Guadeloupe, governed by France.

St Barthelemy: Size: 9.6 square miles. Population: 3,500.

Currency: French franc. 1 franc = approx. 8p; £1 = approx. 12.5 francs.

Language: French.

For more information contact: French Government Tourist Office, 178 Piccadilly, London W1V 0AL, tel. 01-493-7622.

ANGUILLA

Anguilla was part of the British Associated State of St Kitts-Nevis-Anguilla until 1976, when it was granted a separate constitution. It is a self-governed British territory, with its capital at The Valley.

Anguilla: Size: 35 square miles. Population: 7,000.

Currency: Eastern Caribbean dollar. EC $1 = approx. 22p; £1 = approx. EC $4.55.

Language: English.

For more information contact: Anguilla Tourist Office, Suite 21, College House, 29 – 31 Wright's Lane, Kensington, London W8 5SH, tel. 01-937-7725.

SABA

The smallest of the Netherlands Antilles, which also include Sint Maarten, St Eustatius ('Statia') and the islands of Curacao, Aruba and Bonaire off the Venezuelan coast. The Netherlands Antilles, a part of the Kingdom of the Netherlands, have enjoyed full autonomy over internal affairs since 1954.

Saba: Size: 5 square miles. Population: 1,000.

Currency: Netherlands Antilles florin (guilder). 1 florin = approx. 32p; £1 = approx 3.13 florins.

Language: Dutch, English.

ANTIGUA

Antigua and Barbuda gained independence from Great Britain in 1981, and together the two islands are a member of the Commonwealth. The capital is St Johns, Antigua.

Antigua: Size: 108 square miles. Population: 74,000.

Currency: Eastern Caribbean dollar. EC $1 = approx. 22p; £1 = approx. EC $4.55.

Language: English.

For more information contact: Antigua and Barbuda Tourist Office, Antigua House, 15 Thayer Street, London W1M 5LD, tel. 01-486-7073.

MONTSERRAT

Montserrat is a colony of Great Britain, with its capital at Plymouth.

Montserrat: Size: 39.6 square miles. Population: 12,500.

Currency: Eastern Caribbean dollar. EC $1 = approx. 22p; £1 = approx. EC $4.55.

Language: English.

For more information contact: Montserrat Tourist Office, 10 Kensington Court, London W8 5DL, tel. 01-937-9522.

GUADELOUPE

Guadeloupe was colonised by the French in 1635 and remains essentially a French colony, designated a 'Foreign Overseas Department' since the end of World War II and governed from Paris. Other French colonial islands in the Caribbean, including Martinique and St Barthelemy, are subprefectures of Guadeloupe. The capital is Basse-Terre.

Guadeloupe: Size: 687 square miles. Population: 332,000.

Currency: French franc. 1 franc = approx. 8p; £1 = approx. 12.5 francs.

Language: French.

For more information contact: French Government Tourist Office, 178 Piccadilly, London W1V 0AL, tel. 01-493-7622.

DOMINICA

Dominica was colonised by Great Britain in 1805 and gained its independence in 1978. The capital is Roseau.

Dominica: Size: 290 square miles. Population: 70,000.

Currency: Eastern Caribbean dollar. EC $1 = approx. 22p; £1 = approx. EC $4.55.

Languages: English, French patois

For more information contact: Dominica High Commission and Tourist Office, 1 Collingham Gardens, London SW5 0HW, tel. 01-370-5194.

ST LUCIA

Colonial rights to St Lucia were contested between England and
France for over 200 years, until the island officially became a
British colony in 1814. It was granted independence within the
Commonwealth in 1979. Castries is the capital.

St Lucia: Size: 238 square miles. Population: 140,000.

Currency: Eastern Caribbean dollar. EC $1 = approx. 22p; £1
= approx. EC $4.55.

Language: English, French Creole.

For more information contact: St Lucia Tourist Board,
1 Collingham Gardens, London SW5 0HW, tel. 01-370-0926.

BARBADOS

Barbados was colonised by England in 1628 and gained
independence within the Commonwealth in 1966. The Barbados
House of Assembly, at the capital in Bridgetown, is the third
oldest legislative body in the western hemisphere (after Virginia
and the Bahamas).

Barbados: Size: 166 square miles. Population: 257,000.

Currency: Barbados dollar. BD $1 = 29p; £1 = approx. BD
$3.45.

Language: English.

For more information contact: Barbados Board of Tourism,
263 Tottenham Court Road, London W1P 9AA, tel. 01-636-9448.

ST VINCENT & THE GRENADINES

The island of St Vincent is about ten times as large as the
combined land area of the Grenadines — Bequia, Mustique,
Canouan, Palm Island, Union Island and Petit St Vincent.
During its colonial era St Vincent and The Grenadines were
alternately controlled by England and France; they have been
British since 1805. They were granted independence as a member
of the Commonwealth and constitutional monarchy in 1979. The
capital is Scarborough.

St Vincent and The Grenadines: Size: 150 square miles.
Population: 113,000.

Currency: Eastern Caribbean dollar. EC $1 = approx. 22p; £1
= approx. EC $4.55.

Language: English.

For more information contact: St Vincent and The
Grenadines Tourist Office, 1 Collingham Gardens, London SW5
0HW, tel. 01-370-0925.

GRENADA

Grenada and its smaller associated islands, Carriacou and Petit
Martinique, were originally colonised by France in 1674, and

were alternately ruled by the French and the British. It is now an independent nation within the Commonwealth. An attempted coup in 1983 failed after US Marine intervention, and the nation is now considered stable. The capital is St George's.

Grenada: Size: 133 square miles. Population: 110,000.

Currency: Eastern Caribbean dollar. EC $1 = approx. 22p; £1 = approx. EC $4.55.

Language: English.

For more information contact: Grenada National Tourist Office, 1 Collingham Gardens, London SW5 0HW, tel. 01-370-5164.

TRINIDAD AND TOBAGO

The most southerly of the Lesser Antilles chain of islands, Trinidad and Tobago constitute a Republic within the Commonwealth. The capital is Port of Spain, Trinidad.

Trinidad: Size: 1,864 square miles. Population: 1,100,000.

Tobago: Size: 116 square miles. Population: 65,000.

Currency: Trinidad and Tobago dollar. TT $1 = approx 22p; £1 = approx TT $4.55.

Language: English.

For more information contact: Trinidad and Tobago Tourist Board, 48 Leicester Square, London WC2H 7QD, tel. 01-930 6566.

WEST INDIES WORDS

all right a friendly greeting

axst ask

bacchanal confusion, scandal

bad eye antagonism

bazody stupid, confused or foolish

break to avoid doing something

callaloo a soup made from a leafy vegetable similar to spinach

catch me (or you) royal pose a great obstacle

chilibibi parched corn meal mixed with sugar

chicken legs the only part you'll find in West Indian cooking

commess confusion

corbeau vulture

cucoo (or) coo coo a Bajan dish made from ground corn

dolly house mash up collapse or exposure of a scheme

farce (or) fast to pry or stick your nose in others' business

fatigue to tease or heckle

fete party or dance

ganja marijuana

humbug imaginary gremlin blamed for problems (always responsible for power failures and dead phone on Saba)

ital pure food (Rastafarian—no salt, no meat)

Jah God (Rastafarian)

jim boots athletic shoes

johnny cake fried pan bread

jump up party or dance

kaiso calypso

La Diablesse folk spirit, female devil

Lagahoo folk spirit

lambi conch, pounded tender and cooked

lap deer

lime to lounge around doing nothing much

lobsters actually giant crayfish with no claws (delicious when properly prepared)

maco a person who stick his nose into other people's business

macocious nosy

maga scrawny, starving

main man special person

mamaguy to fool or ridicule

mariley a popular West Indian drink made from a root (nasty stuff)

marse (or) mask like a carnival—confusing and/or spectacular

mookman idiot

mountain chicken large Dominican frog legs

nutten nothing

obzokey funny-looking

panorama steel band competition

pati (or) pastiche a little turnover or meat pie, usually filled with salt fish or meat

pelau dish made from rice, peas and meat

plantain thick-skinned green banana, served fried or as a vegetable

put out to be concerned about

raised up brought up as a child

Rasta member of the Rastafarian sect, which originated in Jamaica

reverb electronic sound

roti similar to a burrito, filled with curried chicken, fish, meat or vegetables

sut stupid

teefin stealing (e.g. 'He teefed my goat')

Ting a grapefruit drink

tulum very black sugar cake made from coconut, molasses and sugar

we be jammin we're having a good time

SOUVENIR STRATEGIES

British Virgin Islands: At Pusser's Rum Shop in Tortola, you can buy mugs, ashtrays and clothing with the Pusser's logo. Other good buys are hiking shorts and cookbooks.

St Martin: Paradise Cafe has a good quality T-shirt with an amusing logo. So does Club Orient, along with beach bags, island jewellery, etc. Guavaberry from the West Indian Tavern makes a nice gift. Perfume is inexpensive in St Martin. Fun clothing such as Naf Naf and New Man costs less at New Amsterdam. Around the Bend also has fun cotton clothing and jewellery.

Saba: Take home some Saba lacework—napkins, hankies, etc. Saba Spice is a must. The Island Craft Shop and Artisans Foundation have lots of appealing homemade items. The Square Nickel carries genuine Cuban cigars.

Antigua: Buy a homemade Warri board and get a taxi driver or other local to show you how to play (Joan Salmon is an expert). The game, which originated in Africa, uses 12 scooped-out holes and 24 beads.

Montserrat: Buy a T-shirt or sweatshirt from Air Studios. The Iguana has fun iguana motif jewellery and ashtrays.

Dominica: Plastic shoes like those the Rastas wear are sold here—cheap and waterproof. The bookstore in the town centre has several good cookbooks. The book *Lal Shop* by Paul Keens-Douglas is an intriguing collection of essays, stories and poems written in West Indian dialect for the *Trinidad and Tobago Sunday Express* column, 'Is Town Say So'.

Barbados: If you're on your way home you can take some frozen flying fish! Check at the snack bar outside the airport. Bajan yellow hot sauce and sherry pepper sauce, both available in grocers, make good gifts.

Bequia: Mac's Pizza Parlour has a great T-shirt. The bookstore has one of the best selections of West Indies guides and cookbooks, You can get black coral bracelets and other jewellery on Bequia, Union Island and Grenada. Bargain for these items.

Grenada: Spices are cheap here. A bottle the size of a small Coke bottle or ketchup bottle, full of saffron, is EC $10 (about £2.25). You'll also find the freshest nutmeg you've ever smelled. The baskets used to sort nutmegs are sturdy, made of bent twigs. Check a few days in advance with the spice processing plant and they may be able to get you a new one or sell you one that's in use. Green doctor shirts emblazoned with the name 'St George's Medical School' make a fun memento of the 1984 invasion.

Trinidad: You can buy hot pepper sauce here, as well as an assortment of unusual canned foods.

TRANSPORT INFORMATION

LIAT AIRLINES

LIAT (the acronym stand for 'Leeward Islands Air Transport') offers a bargain that makes island-hopping affordable.

The **LIAT Explorer Fare** costs £85 ($149) for 21 days of inter island travel including three stopovers and return flight to your point of origin. The ticket must be purchased outside the Caribbean, in connection with a BWIA or other air fare to the originating island. You must make firm reservations when you purchase the ticket, and no change of itinerary is allowed afterwards. LIAT tickets can be purchased in the UK through BWIA (see below).

The gateway island, where you start using the LIAT Explorer Fare, can be St Thomas, St Croix, St Maarten, St Kitts, Antigua, St Lucia, Barbados or Trinidad.

Islands you can include as stopovers on the Explorer Fare include Tortola, Anguilla, St Kitts, Nevis, Montserrat, Antigua, Barbuda, Guadeloupe, Martinique, Dominica, St Lucia, Bardados, St Vincent, Mustique, Canouan, Union Island, Carriacou, Grenada and Trinidad.

Liat also offers a **Super Caribbean Explorer Fare,** allowing 30 days of unlimited travel among the islands LIAT serves. The only limitations are that you cannot land at the same airport more than once, and if you change your flight itinerary after ticket purchase you'll be charged an additional £12 ($20) for each flight change.

BRITISH WEST INDIES AIRLINES

You'll get a taste of the West Indies the minute you step aboard a BWIA ('Beewee') flight. Most of their stewardesses and staff come from the airline's home base, Trinidad-Tobago. They have a delightful accent as well as a knack for showing you West Indian hospitality as soon as you sit down.

Meals are chicken and beef choices prepared with a Caribbean flair. We rather look forward to enjoying them, even though we're usually critical of airline 'mystery meals'.

First class is really special, worth the extra expense.

Their in-flight magazine, the *BWIA Sunset,* is full of information on the islands you'll be visiting as well as amusing stories about pirates and the like.

BWIA is also the place to contact in the UK for LIAT reservations. Some BWIA officers also serve on the LIAT board, and BWIA is always aware of LIAT specials such as the Explorer Fares.

Call the BWIA fares department on 01-930 6020 for further information, or the administration department may be able to help with other problems (01-839 7155). Your travel agent will also be able to help.

WINDJAMMER CRUISES

Windjammer has several 'barefoot cruise' options to choose from. Their cruises offer you a chance to see a different island every day and enjoy the experience of sailing on a tall ship, eating well, partying constantly and getting to know an interesting assortment of people.

You can choose from 7, 13 or 19-day cruises at a cost of a little under £60 ($100) a day including your meals and beverages, scuba and snorkelling equipment. Cabins have everything you need for comfort, including air conditioning. You don't need to carry much (in fact, Windjammer says you can literally walk on with just your toothbrush). Their ship store sells everything—shorts, T-shirts, suits, thongs, and even the kit bag to stow it all in.

The *Flying Cloud* tours the British Virgin Islands every week, Monday to Saturday, and is the best choice if scuba diving or snorkelling is your sport. The *Yankee Trader* and the *Polynesia* have different intineraries between St. Martin and Antigua (Monday to Saturday). The *Mandalay,* our favourite, is by far the queen of the fleet. Formerly E.F. Hutton's private yacht, she sails between Antigua and Grenada (alternating directions every two weeks) for 13 days.

The *Barefoot Rogue,* the supply ship for the rest of the Windjammer fleet, sails for 19 days from Freeport in the Bahamas through the West Indies, meeting the other yachts along the way.

Combine a week-long sail on Windjammer with two weeks on land for a perfect Caribbean itinerary. We recommend booking your Windjammer cruise through a travel agent. The relaxed, somewhat disorganised quality that makes the cruise so perfect can infuriate persons dealing with the business office. Your agent can cut through the confusion and receive a commission from them for handling the details.

Your travel agent should be able to get you more information, or alternatively you may write direct to Windjammer Cruises, PO Box 120, Miami Beach, Florida 33119, USA.